THE ARTISAN

MARSHMALLOW

Paige Couture

hardie grant books
MELBOURNE · LONDON

CONTENTS

CHAPTER 1

EASY

♥

Classic Vanilla Marshmallows

MAKES ABOUT 20

515 g (1 lb 2½ oz/2¼ cups) caster (superfine) sugar

1 tablespoon glucose syrup

2 tablespoons powdered gelatine

70 g (2½ oz/2 large) egg whites, at room temperature

2 teaspoons vanilla bean paste or vanilla extract

Coloured sanding sugar to decorate (see Notes)

20 lollipop sticks (see Notes)

COATING

30 g (1 oz/¼ cup) icing (confectioners') sugar

30 g (1 oz/¼ cup) cornflour (cornstarch)

NOTES

Keep in an airtight container for 2–3 days.

These classic marshmallows are delicious tossed in toasted shredded coconut.

Sanding sugar and lollipop sticks are available from specialty cake decorating stores or online.

- Lightly spray a 25 x 30 cm (10 x 12 in) baking tin with oil, line the base and two long sides with non-stick baking paper and lightly spray the paper with oil.

- Combine 460 g (1 lb ¼ oz/2 cups) of the sugar, the glucose and 185 ml (6¼ fl oz/ ¾ cup) water in a small, deep heavy-based saucepan. Stir over low heat until the sugar dissolves. Bring to the boil and simmer, without stirring, until the syrup reaches 127°C (260°F) on a sugar thermometer (this is the upper end of the hard-ball stage). Watch it carefully, as the syrup has a tendency to bubble up.

- Meanwhile, slowly sprinkle the gelatine over 185 ml (6¼ fl oz/¾ cup) cold water in a shallow microwave-safe bowl and set aside for 5 minutes. Heat in the microwave for 30–45 seconds on High (100%), or until the gelatine has dissolved and the liquid is clear.

- When the sugar syrup reaches 115°C (239°F), whisk the egg whites in an electric mixer with a whisk attachment on medium speed. When frothy, increase the speed to medium–high and gradually add the remaining sugar, whisking until thick and glossy. Keep the mixer running on medium speed.

- When the sugar syrup reaches 127°C (260°F), turn off the heat. When the bubbles subside, carefully add the dissolved gelatine – take care, as the mixture may bubble up.

- Increase the mixer speed to medium–high and gradually pour the hot syrup mixture down the inside of the bowl in a thin, steady stream. Increase the speed to high and continue whisking until the mixture is thick. Add the vanilla bean paste or extract and whisk until the mixture is very thick and holds its shape, about 10–12 minutes, depending on your mixer. The outside of the bowl should almost be at room temperature.

- Use a spatula to scrape the marshmallow mixture into the prepared tin and smooth the surface. Stand for 2–3 hours, until set.

- Meanwhile, to make the coating, sift the icing sugar and cornflour together.

- Dust the top of the marshmallow with some of the coating and turn out onto a clean surface. Dust the bottom with more coating. Use a variety of cutters or a large knife sprayed lightly with oil to cut the marshmallow into bite-sized pieces. Roll the sticky sides of each marshmallow in the sanding sugar or toss in the remaining coating, dusting off the excess. Carefully insert the lollipop sticks.

Honey & Almond Marshmallow Cake

MAKES 1 LARGE CAKE OR ABOUT 35

- Lightly spray four 20 cm (8 in) round cake tins with oil and line the bases with non-stick baking paper. Combine 345 g (12 oz/1½ cups) of the sugar, the honey and 125 ml (4 fl oz/½ cup) water in a medium, deep heavy-based saucepan. Stir over low heat until the sugar dissolves. Bring to the boil and simmer, without stirring, until the syrup reaches 127°C (260°F) on a sugar thermometer (this is the upper end of the hard-ball stage). Watch it carefully, as the syrup has a tendency to bubble up.

- Meanwhile, slowly sprinkle the gelatine over 160 ml (5¼ fl oz/⅔ cup) cold water in a shallow microwave-safe bowl and set aside for 5 minutes. Heat in the microwave for 30–45 seconds on High (100%), or until the gelatine has dissolved and the liquid is clear.

- When the sugar syrup reaches 115°C (239°F), whisk the egg whites in an electric mixer with a whisk attachment on medium speed. When frothy, increase the speed to medium–high and gradually add the remaining sugar, whisking until thick and glossy. Keep the mixer running on medium speed.

- When the sugar syrup reaches 127°C (260°F), turn off the heat and allow the bubbles to subside.

- Increase the mixer speed to medium–high and gradually pour the gelatine mixture down the inside of the bowl in a thin, steady stream. Add the hot sugar syrup in the same manner. Increase the speed to high and continue whisking until the mixture is very thick and holds its shape, about 10–12 minutes, depending on your mixer. The outside of the bowl should almost be at room temperature.

- Use a spatula to scrape the marshmallow mixture into the prepared tins and smooth the surface. Sprinkle with one-third of the almonds. Stand for 2–3 hours, until set.

- Carefully turn the marshmallows out of the tins and layer with the remaining almonds on a cake stand.

180 g (6¼ oz/2 cups) flaked almonds, toasted
400 g (14 oz/1¾ cups) caster (superfine) sugar
175 g (6 oz/½ cup) honey
2 tablespoons powdered gelatine
70 g (2½ oz/2 large) egg whites, at room temperature

NOTES

Keep in an airtight container for 2–3 days.

Try using different honey types in this recipe.

If you would prefer, set the marshmallows in a 25 x 30 cm (10 x 12 in) baking tin. Lightly spray with oil and line the base and two long sides with non-stick baking paper. Cut the set marshmallow into pieces and toss in the almonds.

Marshmallow Liquorice Allsorts

MAKES ABOUT 35

515 g (1 lb 2½ oz/2¼ cups) caster (superfine) sugar

1 tablespoon glucose syrup

2 tablespoons powdered gelatine

70 g (2½ oz/2 large) egg whites, at room temperature

2 teaspoons vanilla bean paste or vanilla extract

8–10 drops raspberry oil flavouring (see Notes)

Pink food colouring

1 quantity Liquorice marshmallow twist mixture (page 82)

COATING

30 g (1 oz/¼ cup) icing (confectioners') sugar

30 g (1 oz/¼ cup) cornflour (cornstarch)

NOTES

Keep in an airtight container for 2–3 days.

Raspberry oil flavouring is available from specialty cake decorating stores or online.

Don't be shy when adding colour to the marshmallow mixtures!

- Lightly spray two 25 x 30 cm (10 x 12 in) slice tins with oil and line the base and two long sides of each with non-stick baking paper. Lightly spray the paper of one tin with oil and leave the other unsprayed.

- Combine 460 g (1 lb ¼ oz/2 cups) of the sugar, the glucose and 185 ml (6¼ fl oz/¾ cup) water in a small, deep heavy-based saucepan. Stir over low heat until the sugar dissolves. Bring to the boil and simmer, without stirring, until the syrup reaches 127°C (260°F) on a sugar thermometer (this is the upper end of the hard-ball stage). Watch it carefully, as the syrup has a tendency to bubble up.

- Meanwhile, slowly sprinkle the gelatine over 185 ml (6¼ fl oz/¾ cup) cold water in a shallow microwave-safe bowl and set aside for 5 minutes. Heat in a microwave for 30–45 seconds on High (100%), or until the gelatine has dissolved.

- When the sugar syrup reaches 115°C (239°F), whisk the egg whites in an electric mixer with a whisk attachment on medium speed. When frothy, increase the speed to medium–high and gradually add the remaining sugar, whisking until thick and glossy. Keep the mixer running on medium speed.

- When the syrup reaches 127°C (260°F), turn off the heat and allow the bubbles to subside.

- Increase the mixer speed to medium–high and pour the gelatine mixture down the inside of the bowl in a thin, steady stream. Add the hot sugar syrup in the same manner. Increase the speed to high and continue whisking until the mixture is thick. Add the vanilla and whisk until the mixture is very thick and holds its shape, about 10–12 minutes. The outside of the bowl should almost be at room temperature.

- Use a spatula to scrape half the marshmallow mixture into the tin with the unsprayed paper and, working quickly, smooth the surface. Return the bowl to the mixer stand and whisk in the raspberry oil and food colouring until combined. Scrape the raspberry mixture into the tin with the sprayed paper and smooth the surface.

- Prepare the Liquorice marshmallow mixture as instructed and spread evenly over the raspberry marshmallow. Stand for 1–2 hours, until set.

- Meanwhile, to make the coating, sift the sugar and cornflour together. Invert the vanilla marshmallow onto the liquorice marshmallow. They should hold together. Dust the top of the marshmallow with some of the coating and turn out onto a surface. Dust the bottom with more coating. Use a hot knife or cutters to cut the marshmallow into bite-sized pieces. Toss the marshmallow pieces in the remaining coating, dusting off the excess.

Mocha Latte Marshmallow

Mocha Latte Marshmallow

Mocha Latte Marshmallow

Mocha Latte Marshmallow

Mocha Latte Marshmallows

- Lightly spray a 20 x 30 cm (8 x 12 in) slice tin with oil, line the base and two long sides with non-stick baking paper and lightly spray the paper with oil.

- Combine 460 g (1 lb ¼ oz/2 cups) of the sugar, the glucose and 185 ml (6¼ fl oz/¾ cup) water in a small, deep heavy-based saucepan. Stir over low heat until the sugar dissolves. Bring to the boil and simmer, without stirring, until the syrup reaches 121°C (250°F) on a sugar thermometer (hard-ball stage). Watch it carefully, as the syrup has a tendency to bubble up.

- Meanwhile, dissolve the coffee in a tablespoon of hot water, then put in a microwave-safe bowl with enough hot water to make 185 ml (6¼ fl oz/¾ cup). Slowly sprinkle over the gelatine and set aside for 5 minutes. Heat in the microwave for 30–45 seconds on High (100%), or until the gelatine has dissolved.

- When the sugar syrup reaches 112°C (234°F), whisk the egg whites in an electric mixer with a whisk attachment on medium speed. When frothy, increase the speed to medium–high and gradually add the remaining sugar, whisking until thick and glossy. Keep the mixer running on medium speed.

- When the sugar syrup reaches 121°C (250°F), turn off the heat. When the bubbles subside, carefully add the dissolved gelatine – take care, as the mixture may bubble up.

- Increase the mixer speed to medium–high and gradually pour the hot syrup mixture down the inside of the bowl in a thin, steady stream. Increase the speed to high and continue whisking until the mixture is very thick and holds its shape, about 10–12 minutes, depending on your mixer. The outside of the bowl should almost be at room temperature.

- Pour two-thirds of the marshmallow mixture into the prepared tin and smooth the surface. Fold the chocolate into the remaining mixture until melted and just combined, then pour over the coffee marshmallow and spread evenly. Stand for 2–3 hours, until set.

- Meanwhile, to make the coating, sift the icing sugar and cornflour together.

- Dust the top of the marshmallow with some of the coating and turn out onto a clean surface. Dust the bottom with more coating. Use a 3.5 cm (1½ in) cutter sprayed lightly with oil to cut the marshmallow into rounds. Roll the sticky sides of each marshmallow in the crushed candy.

515 g (1 lb 2½ oz/2¼ cups) caster (superfine) sugar

1 tablespoon glucose syrup

1 tablespoon instant espresso coffee granules (see Notes)

2 tablespoons powdered gelatine

70 g (2½ oz/2 large) egg whites, at room temperature

50 g (1¾ oz) dark chocolate, grated

150 g (5½ oz) coffee candy, roughly crushed (see Notes)

COATING

2 tablespoons icing (confectioners') sugar

2 tablespoons cornflour (cornstarch)

NOTES

Keep in an airtight container for 2–3 days.

If you have a coffee machine, replace the coffee granules with 185 ml (6¼ fl oz/¾ cup) freshly made strong black coffee.

Coffee candy is available from Asian grocery stores.

Peppermint Marshmallows

MAKES ABOUT 20

- Lightly spray a 25 x 30 cm (10 x 12 in) baking tin with oil, line the base and two long sides with non-stick baking paper and lightly spray the paper with oil.

- Combine 460 g (1 lb ¼ oz/2 cups) of the sugar, the glucose and 185 ml (6¼ fl oz/ ¾ cup) water in a small, deep heavy-based saucepan. Stir over low heat until the sugar dissolves. Bring to the boil and simmer, without stirring, until the syrup reaches 127°C (260°F) on a sugar thermometer (this is the upper end of the hard-ball stage). Watch it carefully, as the syrup has a tendency to bubble up.

- Meanwhile, slowly sprinkle the gelatine over 185 ml (6¼ fl oz/¾ cup) cold water in a shallow microwave-safe bowl and set aside for 5 minutes. Heat in the microwave for 30–45 seconds on High (100%), or until the gelatine has dissolved and the liquid is clear.

- When the sugar syrup reaches 115°C (239°F), whisk the egg whites in an electric mixer with a whisk attachment on medium speed. When soft peaks form, increase the speed to medium–high and gradually add the remaining sugar. Keep the mixer running on medium speed.

- When the sugar syrup reaches 127°C (260°F), turn off the heat. When the bubbles subside, carefully add the dissolved gelatine – take care, as the mixture may bubble up.

- Increase the mixer speed to medium–high and gradually pour the hot syrup mixture down the inside of the bowl in a thin, steady stream. Increase the speed to high and continue whisking until the mixture is thick. Add the peppermint oil and whisk until the mixture is very thick and holds its shape, about 10–12 minutes, depending on your mixer. The outside of the bowl should almost be at room temperature.

- Add about 10 drops of food colouring to the marshmallow mixture and gently fold through just 2–3 times. Use a spatula to scrape the mixture into the prepared tin and smooth the surface. Swirl a couple of extra drops of colouring through the top of the marshmallow, if you like. Stand for 2–3 hours, until set.

- Meanwhile, to make the coating, sift the icing sugar and cornflour together.

- Dust the top of the marshmallow lightly with some of the coating and turn out onto a clean surface. Dust the bottom with more coating, dusting off any excess. Use a 5.5 cm (2¼ in) cutter sprayed lightly with oil to cut the marshmallow into rounds. Close to serving time, roll the sticky sides of each marshmallow in the crushed chocolate bars.

515 g (1 lb 2½ oz/2¼ cups) caster (superfine) sugar
1 tablespoon glucose syrup
2 tablespoons powdered gelatine
70 g (2½ oz/2 large) egg whites, at room temperature
3–4 drops peppermint oil, or to taste (see Notes)
Green food colouring
2 x 35 g (1¼ oz) mint chocolate bars, crushed (such as Peppermint Crisp)

COATING
2 tablespoons icing (confectioners') sugar
2 tablespoons cornflour (cornstarch)

NOTES
Keep in an airtight container for 1–2 days.

Flavoured oils are extremely potent – add them with caution!

Try folding 75 g (2½ oz) roughly chopped dark chocolate through the mixture before pouring it into the tin.

You can also make these marshmallows in ice cream cone cups, as in the photograph. Fill a large piping bag fitted with a star tube with marshmallow and pipe into 24 cups. Sprinkle with chocolate before serving.

CHAPTER 2

FRUITY

Apple, Cinnamon & Rose Marshmallows

MAKES ABOUT 40

- Lightly spray a 25 x 30 cm (10 x 12 in) baking tin with oil, line the base and two long sides with non-stick baking paper and lightly spray the paper with oil. Or, lightly spray 3 large baking trays with oil. To make the coating, sift the icing sugar and cornflour together. Dust some of the coating over the trays.

- Combine 460 g (1 lb ¼ oz/2 cups) of the sugar, the glucose, berries, cinnamon stick and 185 ml (6¼ fl oz/¾ cup) water in a small, deep heavy-based saucepan. Stir over low heat until the sugar dissolves. Bring to the boil and simmer, without stirring, until the syrup reaches 127°C (260°F) on a sugar thermometer (this is the upper end of the hard-ball stage). Watch it carefully, as the syrup has a tendency to bubble up.

- Meanwhile, slowly sprinkle the gelatine over 160 ml (5¼ fl oz/⅔ cup) cold water in a shallow microwave-safe bowl and set aside for 5 minutes. Heat in the microwave for 30–45 seconds on High (100%), or until the gelatine has dissolved.

- When the sugar syrup reaches 115°C (239°F), whisk the egg whites in an electric mixer with a whisk attachment on medium speed. When frothy, increase the speed to medium–high and gradually add the remaining sugar, whisking until thick and glossy. Keep the mixer running on medium speed.

- When the sugar syrup reaches 127°C (260°F), turn off the heat and allow the bubbles to subside. Remove the berries and cinnamon stick with a slotted spoon and discard. Carefully add the dissolved gelatine – take care, as the mixture may bubble up.

- Increase the mixer speed to medium–high and gradually pour the hot syrup mixture down the inside of the bowl in a thin, steady stream. Increase the speed to high and continue whisking until the mixture is thick. Add the apple juice concentrate, rosewater and ground cinnamon, and whisk until the mixture is very thick and holds its shape, about 10–12 minutes, depending on your mixer. The outside of the bowl should almost be at room temperature.

- Use a spatula to scrape the marshmallow mixture into the prepared rectangular tin and smooth the surface. Or, dollop large spoonfuls of the marshmallow mixture onto the prepared trays and sprinkle with the rose petals. Stand for 1–2 hours, until set.

- Once set, turn the rectangular marshmallow out onto a clean surface and cut into rounds with a small cutter sprayed lightly with oil. Toss half of these marshmallows in rose petals and the remaining in the coating mixture. Attach to the cake with toothpicks, if desired.

515 g (1 lb 2½ oz/2¼ cups) caster (superfine) sugar
1 tablespoon glucose syrup
6 juniper berries
1 cinnamon stick
2 tablespoons powdered gelatine
70 g (2½ oz/2 large) egg whites, at room temperature
2 tablespoons apple juice concentrate (see Notes)
¼ teaspoon rosewater (see Notes)
¼ teaspoon ground cinnamon
2 tablespoons dried rose petals
Large tiered cake for decorating, if desired

COATING

2 tablespoons icing (confectioners') sugar
2 tablespoons cornflour (cornstarch)

NOTES

Keep in an airtight container for 2–3 days.

Apple juice concentrate is available in the health food aisle of supermarkets.

Rosewater is available from Middle Eastern or gourmet grocery stores. It varies in strength, so don't overdo it!

Double Raspberry Marshmallows

MAKES ABOUT 24

330 g (11½ oz) frozen raspberries, thawed

515 g (1 lb 2½ oz/2¼ cups) caster (superfine) sugar

1 tablespoon glucose syrup

1½ tablespoons powdered gelatine

70 g (2½ oz/2 large) egg whites, at room temperature

RASPBERRY SUGAR COATING

110 g (3¾ oz/½ cup) raw (demerara) sugar

NOTES

Keep in an airtight container for 2–3 days.

- Lightly spray a 20 x 30 cm (8 x 12 in) slice tin with oil, line the base and two long sides with non-stick baking paper and lightly spray the paper with oil. Purée the raspberries, then strain through a fine sieve and discard the seeds. You will need 220 ml (7½ fl oz) raspberry purée for this recipe.

- Combine 460 g (1 lb ¼ oz/2 cups) of the sugar, the glucose and 185 ml (6¼ fl oz/¾ cup) water in a small, deep heavy-based saucepan. Stir over low heat until the sugar dissolves. Bring to the boil and simmer, without stirring, until the syrup reaches 121°C (250°F) on a sugar thermometer (hard-ball stage). Watch it carefully, as the syrup has a tendency to bubble up.

- Meanwhile, slowly sprinkle the gelatine over 200 ml (7 fl oz) of the raspberry purée in a shallow microwave-safe bowl and whisk to combine. Set aside for 5 minutes. Heat in the microwave for 30–45 seconds on High (100%), or until the gelatine has dissolved.

- When the sugar syrup reaches 112°C (234°F), whisk the egg whites in an electric mixer with a whisk attachment on medium speed. When frothy, increase the speed to medium–high and gradually add the remaining sugar, whisking until thick and glossy. Keep the mixer running on medium speed.

- When the sugar syrup reaches 121°C (250°F), turn off the heat. When the bubbles subside, carefully add the gelatine mixture – take care, as the syrup may bubble up.

- Increase the mixer speed to medium–high and gradually pour the hot syrup mixture down the inside of the bowl in a thin, steady stream. Increase the speed to high and whisk until the mixture is very thick and holds its shape, about 6–8 minutes, depending on your mixer. The outside of the bowl should almost be at room temperature.

- Use a spatula to scrape the marshmallow mixture into the prepared tin and smooth the surface. Stand for 2–3 hours, until set.

- Meanwhile, to make the raspberry sugar coating, preheat the oven to 110°C (230°F) and line a baking tray with non-stick baking paper. Combine the sugar and the remaining raspberry purée in a small bowl. Spread over the prepared tray and cook for 40–45 minutes or until dry. Remove from the oven and allow to cool. Crumble the raspberry sugar if clumps have formed.

Turn the marshmallow out onto a clean surface and cut into shapes with cutters or a large knife sprayed lightly with oil. Roll in the raspberry sugar.

Fresh Ginger & Lemon Marshmallows

MAKES ABOUT 24

515 g (1 lb 2½ oz/2¼ cups) caster (superfine) sugar

1 tablespoon glucose syrup

2 tablespoons powdered gelatine

70 g (2½ oz/2 large) egg whites, at room temperature

1 teaspoon finely grated ginger

1 teaspoon finely grated lemon zest

50 g (1¾ oz) glacé ginger, finely sliced (optional)

Decorative letters to decorate, if desired

NOTE

Keep in an airtight container for 2–3 days.

- Lightly spray a 25 x 30 cm (10 x 12 in) baking tin with oil, line the base and two long sides with non-stick baking paper and lightly spray the paper with oil. Combine 460 g (1 lb ¼ oz/2 cups) of the sugar, the glucose and 185 ml (6¼ fl oz/¾ cup) water in a small, deep heavy-based saucepan. Stir over low heat until the sugar dissolves. Bring to the boil and simmer, without stirring, until the syrup reaches 127°C (260°F) on a sugar thermometer (this is the upper end of the hard-ball stage). Watch it carefully, as the syrup has a tendency to bubble up.

- Meanwhile, slowly sprinkle the gelatine over 185 ml (6¼ fl oz/¾ cup) cold water in a shallow microwave-safe bowl and set aside for 5 minutes. Heat in the microwave for 30–45 seconds on High (100%), or until the gelatine has dissolved and the liquid is clear.

- When the sugar syrup reaches 115°C (239°F), whisk the egg whites in an electric mixer with a whisk attachment on medium speed. When frothy, increase the speed to medium–high and gradually add the remaining sugar, whisking until thick and glossy. Keep the mixer running on medium speed.

- When the sugar syrup reaches 127°C (260°F), turn off the heat and allow the bubbles to subside.

- Increase the mixer speed to medium–high and gradually pour the gelatine mixture down the inside of the bowl in a thin, steady stream. Add the hot sugar syrup in the same manner. Increase the speed to high and continue whisking until the mixture is thick. Add the ginger and lemon zest and whisk until the mixture is very thick and holds its shape, about 10–12 minutes, depending on your mixer. The outside of the bowl should almost be at room temperature.

- Use a spatula to scrape the marshmallow mixture into the prepared tin and smooth the surface. Stand for 2–3 hours until set.

- Use a large knife sprayed lightly with oil to cut the marshmallow into bite-sized pieces. Top with decorative letters or sprinkle with the glacé ginger if using.

Lemon & Vanilla Marshmallows with Basil Sugar

MAKES ABOUT 35

515 g (1 lb 2½ oz/2¼ cups) caster (superfine) sugar

1 tablespoon glucose syrup

2 tablespoons powdered gelatine

70 g (2½ oz/2 large) egg whites, at room temperature

1 teaspoon finely grated lemon zest

2 vanilla beans, split lengthwise and seeds scraped, or 1 teaspoon vanilla bean paste

BASIL SUGAR COATING

110 g (3¾ oz/½ cup) raw (demerara) sugar

2 tablespoons firmly packed basil leaves

2 tablespoons icing (confectioners') sugar

2 tablespoons cornflour (cornstarch)

NOTE

Keep in an airtight container for 2–3 days.

- Spray a 25 x 30 cm (10 x 12 in) baking tin with oil, line the base and sides with non-stick baking paper and spray the paper with oil. Combine 460 g (1 lb ¼ oz/2 cups) of the sugar, the glucose and 185 ml (6¼ fl oz/¾ cup) water in a small, deep heavy-based saucepan. Stir over low heat until the sugar dissolves. Bring to the boil and simmer, without stirring, until the syrup reaches 127°C (260°F) on a sugar thermometer (the upper end of the hard-ball stage). Watch it carefully, as the syrup has a tendency to bubble up.

- Meanwhile, slowly sprinkle the gelatine over 185 ml (6¼ fl oz/¾ cup) cold water in a shallow microwave-safe bowl and set aside for 5 minutes. Heat in the microwave for 30–45 seconds on High (100%), or until the gelatine has dissolved.

- When the sugar syrup reaches 115°C (239°F), whisk the egg whites in a mixer with a whisk attachment on medium speed. When frothy, increase the speed to medium–high and gradually add the remaining sugar, whisking until thick and glossy. Keep the mixer running on medium speed. When the sugar syrup reaches 127°C (260°F), turn off the heat. When the bubbles subside, carefully add the dissolved gelatine – take care, as the mixture may bubble up.

- Increase the mixer speed to medium–high and gradually pour the hot syrup mixture down the inside of the bowl in a thin, steady stream. Increase the speed to high and continue whisking until the mixture is thick. Add the lemon zest and vanilla seeds or paste and whisk until the mixture is very thick and holds its shape, about 10–12 minutes, depending on your mixer. The outside of the bowl should almost be at room temperature.

- Use a spatula to scrape the marshmallow mixture into the prepared tin and smooth the surface. Stand for 2–3 hours, until set.

- Meanwhile, to make the basil sugar coating, preheat the oven to 110°C (230°F) and line a baking tray with non-stick baking paper. Put the sugar and basil in a small food processor and pulse briefly until just combined. Do not over-process. Spread over the prepared tray and cook for 12–15 minutes or until dry. Remove from the oven and allow to cool. Crumble the basil sugar if clumps have formed. In a separate bowl, sift the icing sugar and cornflour together for the coating. Dust the top of the marshmallow with some of the coating and turn out onto a clean surface. Dust the bottom with more coating, dusting off the excess. Use a large knife sprayed lightly with oil to cut the marshmallow into bite-sized pieces. Roll the sticky sides of each marshmallow piece in the basil sugar.

Maple & Orange Marshmallows

MAKES ABOUT 24

- Lightly spray a 20 x 30 cm (8 x 12 in) slice tin with oil, line the base and two long sides with non-stick baking paper and lightly spray the paper with oil.

- Combine 400 g (14 oz/1¾ cups) of the sugar, the glucose and 185 ml (6¼ fl oz/¾ cup) water in a small, deep heavy-based saucepan. Stir over low heat until the sugar dissolves. Bring to the boil and simmer, without stirring, until the syrup reaches 116°C (241°F) on a sugar thermometer (soft-ball stage). Watch it carefully, as the syrup has a tendency to bubble up.

- Meanwhile, slowly sprinkle the gelatine over the orange juice in a shallow microwave-safe bowl and set aside for 5 minutes. Heat in the microwave for 30–45 seconds on High (100%), or until the gelatine has dissolved.

- When the sugar syrup reaches 108°C (226°F), whisk the egg whites in an electric mixer with a whisk attachment on medium speed. When frothy, increase the speed to medium–high and gradually add the remaining sugar, whisking until thick and glossy. Keep the mixer running on medium speed.

- When the sugar syrup reaches 116°C (241°F), turn off the heat and allow the bubbles to subside.

- Increase the mixer speed to medium–high and gradually pour the gelatine mixture down the inside of the bowl in a thin, steady stream. Add the hot sugar syrup in the same manner. Increase the speed to high and continue whisking until the mixture is thick. Gradually add the orange zest and maple syrup and continue to whisk until the mixture is very thick and holds its shape, about 10–12 minutes, depending on your mixer. The outside of the bowl should almost be at room temperature.

- Use a spatula to scrape the marshmallow mixture into the prepared tin and smooth the surface. Stand for 2–3 hours, until set.

- Meanwhile, to make the coating, mix the sugar and spice together. Use a 6.5 cm (2½ in) cutter sprayed lightly with oil to cut the marshmallow into rounds, then cut some of the rounds in half to form wedges. Toss the marshmallow pieces in the coating, dusting off the excess.

460 g (1 lb ¼ oz/2 cups) raw caster (superfine) sugar
1 tablespoon glucose syrup
1½ tablespoons powdered gelatine
160 ml (5¼ fl oz/⅔ cup) strained freshly squeezed orange juice
70 g (2½ oz/2 large) egg whites, at room temperature
½ teaspoon finely grated orange zest
80 ml (2½ fl oz/⅓ cup) pure maple syrup

SUGAR SPICE COATING
75 g (2½ oz/⅓ cup) sugar
½ teaspoon mixed (pumpkin pie) spice

NOTE
Keep in an airtight container for 2–3 days.

Passionfruit Snowballs

MAKES 24

10 passionfruit, halved
515 g (1 lb 2½ oz/2¼ cups)
   caster (superfine) sugar
1 tablespoon glucose syrup
1½ tablespoons powdered
   gelatine
70 g (2½ oz/2 large) egg
   whites, at room temperature

COATING

180 g (6¼ oz/3 cups) shredded
   coconut, toasted

NOTES

*Keep in an airtight container
for 1–2 days.*

*If you have some marshmallow
mixture left over, you can spoon
or pipe dollops onto a lightly
oiled tray or spread over the
base of a small pan to set.*

*Add a few drops of yellow
food colouring if you'd like
to intensify the 'passionfruit'
colour.*

- Lightly spray four 12-hole round-based gem irons, 30 ml (1 fl oz) silicon baking moulds or 30 ml (1 fl oz) mini muffin pans with oil. Scoop the passionfruit pulp into a sieve set over a shallow microwave-safe bowl to catch the juice. Discard the seeds. You will need 200 ml (7 fl oz) of juice for this recipe. If you do not have quite enough juice, make up the difference with water.

- Combine 460 g (1 lb ¼ oz/2 cups) of the sugar, the glucose and 185 ml (6¼ fl oz/¾ cup) water in a small, deep heavy-based saucepan. Stir over low heat until the sugar dissolves. Bring to the boil and simmer, without stirring, until the syrup reaches 121°C (250°F) on a sugar thermometer (hard-ball stage). Watch it carefully, as the syrup has a tendency to bubble up.

- Meanwhile, slowly sprinkle the gelatine over the passionfruit juice and set aside for 5 minutes. Heat in the microwave for 30–45 seconds on High (100%), or until the gelatine has dissolved.

- When the sugar syrup reaches 112°C (234°F), whisk the egg whites in an electric mixer with a whisk attachment on medium speed. When frothy, increase the speed to medium–high and gradually add the remaining sugar, whisking until thick and glossy. Keep the mixer running on medium speed.

- When the sugar syrup reaches 121°C (250°F), turn off the heat. When the bubbles subside, carefully add the gelatine mixture – take care, as the syrup may bubble up.

- Increase the mixer speed to medium–high and gradually pour the hot syrup mixture down the inside of the bowl in a thin, steady stream. Increase the speed to high and continue whisking until the mixture is very thick and holds its shape, about 8–10 minutes, depending on your mixer. The outside of the bowl should almost be at room temperature.

- Spoon or pipe the marshmallow mixture into the oiled moulds, ensuring the surface of each is flat. Stand for 2–3 hours, until firm but sticky.

- Slide 2 marshmallows out of their moulds and sandwich together. They should be sticky enough to join together securely. Repeat with the remaining marshmallows, then roll in the coconut to cover completely.

Raspberry Marshmallow Lamingtons

MAKES ABOUT 35 MEDIUM OR 80 SMALL

- Lightly spray a 20 x 30 cm (8 x 12 in) slice tin with oil, line the base and two long sides with non-stick baking paper and lightly spray the paper with oil. Purée the raspberries, then strain through a fine sieve into a shallow microwave-safe bowl and discard the seeds. You will need 200 ml (7 fl oz) purée for this recipe.

- Combine 460 g (1 lb ¼ oz/2 cups) of the sugar, the glucose and 185 ml (6¼ fl oz/¾ cup) water in a small, deep heavy-based saucepan. Stir over low heat until the sugar dissolves. Bring to the boil and simmer, without stirring, until the syrup reaches 121°C (250°F) on a sugar thermometer (hard-ball stage). Watch it carefully, as the syrup has a tendency to bubble up.

- Meanwhile, slowly sprinkle the gelatine over the raspberry purée and whisk to combine. Set aside for 5 minutes. Heat in the microwave for 30–45 seconds on High (100%), or until the gelatine has dissolved.

- When the syrup reaches 112°C (234°F), whisk the egg whites in an electric mixer with a whisk attachment on medium speed. When frothy, increase the speed to medium–high and gradually add the remaining sugar, whisking until thick and glossy. Keep the mixer running on medium speed.

- When the sugar syrup reaches 121°C (250°F), turn off the heat. When the bubbles subside, carefully add the gelatine mixture – take care, as the syrup may bubble up.

- Increase the mixer speed to medium–high and gradually pour the hot syrup mixture down the inside of the bowl in a thin, steady stream. Increase the speed to high and whisk until the mixture is very thick and holds its shape, about 6–8 minutes. The outside of the bowl should almost be at room temperature. Use a spatula to scrape the marshmallow mixture into the prepared tin and smooth the surface. Stand for 3–4 hours, until set. Meanwhile, to make the coating, sift the icing sugar and cornflour together.

- Turn the marshmallow out onto a clean surface. Use a large knife sprayed with oil to cut the marshmallow into cubes. Toss the marshmallow cubes in the coating, dusting off the excess. Spread the coconut over a tray and place a wire rack over another tray.

- To make the glaze, stir the milk and butter in a medium saucepan over low heat until the butter has melted. Remove from the heat and whisk in the sifted icing sugar and cocoa until smooth. Dunk each marshmallow cube in the glaze, turning with a fork. Remove and place on the wire rack briefly while the excess glaze drips off. Roll in the coconut and set aside for about 30 minutes, or until the chocolate has set.

330 g (11½ oz) frozen raspberries, thawed
515 g (1 lb 2½ oz/2¼ cups) caster (superfine) sugar
1 tablespoon glucose syrup
1½ tablespoons powdered gelatine
70 g (2½ oz/2 large) egg whites, at room temperature
120 g (4 oz/2 cups) shredded coconut

COATING
30 g (1 oz/¼ cup) icing (confectioners') sugar
30 g (1 oz/¼ cup) cornflour (cornstarch)

CHOCOLATE GLAZE
160 ml (5¼ fl oz/⅔ cup) milk
25 g (1 oz) butter
500 g (1 lb 2 oz/4 cups) icing (confectioners') sugar
60 g (2¼ oz/½ cup) Dutch (unsweetened) cocoa powder

NOTES
Keep in an airtight container for 1–2 days.

This glaze can be used to coat any marshmallows you like. The passionfruit and chocolate varieties work particularly well.

CHAPTER 3

❀ SWIRLY ❀

Citrus Swirl Marshmallows

MAKES ABOUT 35

- To make the curd, put the butter, zest and juice in a microwave-safe bowl. Cook on High (100%) for 2 minutes. Stir in the sugar and cook for a further 90 seconds. Gradually whisk in the eggs. Cook on Medium–low (30%), stirring every 2 minutes, until the mixture thickens, about 8–10 minutes. Do not allow the mixture to boil. Leave to cool.

- Lightly spray a 25 x 30 cm (10 x 12 in) baking tin with oil, line the base and two long sides with non-stick baking paper and lightly spray the paper with oil.

- Prepare the marshmallow mixture – you need to vary the technique slightly, as follows, to give a slightly firmer marshmallow. When the sugar syrup reaches 127°C (260°F), turn off the heat and allow the bubbles to subside. Do not add the gelatine mixture to the sugar syrup. Increase the mixer speed to medium–high and gradually pour the gelatine mixture down the inside of the bowl in a thin, steady stream. Add the hot sugar syrup in the same manner. Continue whisking as instructed, until the mixture is very thick and holds its shape.

- Add a small scoop of marshmallow mixture to the cooled curd and mix well. Reserve a couple of tablespoons of the curd mixture and use a large spoon or spatula to gently fold the rest through the marshmallow, stirring and lifting the mixture only 2–3 times. Do not over-mix.

- Use a spatula to scrape the marshmallow mixture into the prepared tin and gently smooth it out. Swirl the reserved curd through the top of the marshmallow. Stand for 2–3 hours, until set.

- Meanwhile, to make the coating, sift the icing sugar and cornflour together.

- Use the overhanging baking paper to lift the marshmallow out of the tin. Use a large knife sprayed lightly with oil to cut it into pieces. Gently dust the marshmallow pieces in the coating if you find them too sticky to handle.

1 quantity Classic vanilla marshmallow mixture (page 8)

EASY LEMON AND LIME CURD
60 g (2¼ oz) butter, chopped
1 lime, zest finely grated
1 lemon, zest finely grated
60 ml (2 fl oz/¼ cup) freshly squeezed lemon and lime juice, strained
115 g (4 oz/½ cup) caster (superfine) sugar
2 large eggs, lightly beaten

COATING
30 g (1 oz/¼ cup) icing (confectioners') sugar
30 g (1 oz/¼ cup) cornflour (cornstarch)

NOTES
Keep in an airtight container for 2–3 days.

This delicious marshmallow is a little bit oozy so it requires patience when dusting in the coating, but it's definitely worth the effort!

Honey & Peanut Butter Swirl Marshmallows

MAKES ABOUT 35

400 g (14 oz/1¾ cups)
    caster (superfine) sugar
150 g (5 oz) honey
2 tablespoons powdered
    gelatine
70 g (2½ oz/2 large) egg
    whites, at room temperature
185 g (6½ oz/¾ cup) crunchy
    peanut butter

COATING

30 g (1 oz/¼ cup) icing
    (confectioners') sugar
30 g (1 oz/¼ cup) cornflour
    (cornstarch)

NOTE

*Keep in an airtight container
for 2–3 days.*

- Lightly spray a 25 x 30 cm (10 x 12 in) baking tin with oil, line the base and two long sides with non-stick baking paper and lightly spray the paper with oil. Combine 345 g (12 oz/1½ cups) of the sugar, the honey and 125 ml (4 fl oz/½ cup) water in a medium, deep heavy-based saucepan. Stir over low heat until the sugar dissolves. Bring to the boil and simmer, without stirring, until the syrup reaches 127°C (260°F) on a sugar thermometer (this is the upper end of the hard-ball stage). Watch it carefully, as the syrup has a tendency to bubble up.

- Meanwhile, slowly sprinkle the gelatine over 160 ml (5¼ fl oz/⅔ cup) cold water in a shallow microwave-safe bowl and set aside for 5 minutes. Heat in the microwave for 30–45 seconds on High (100%), or until the gelatine has dissolved.

- When the sugar syrup reaches 115°C (239°F), whisk the egg whites in an electric mixer with a whisk attachment on medium speed. When frothy, increase the speed to medium–high and gradually add the remaining sugar, whisking until thick and glossy. Keep the mixer running on medium speed. When the sugar syrup reaches 127°C (260°F), turn off the heat and allow the bubbles to subside.

- Increase the mixer speed to medium–high and gradually pour the gelatine mixture down the inside of the bowl in a thin, steady stream. Add the hot sugar syrup in the same manner. Increase the speed to high and whisk until the mixture is very thick and holds its shape, about 10–12 minutes, depending on your mixer. The outside of the bowl should almost be at room temperature.

- Meanwhile, put the peanut butter in a small microwave-safe bowl and heat in the microwave on Medium (50%) in 15-second bursts until softened slightly, but not hot.

- Reserve a couple of tablespoons of the peanut butter and use a large spoon or spatula to gently fold the rest through the marshmallow mixture, stirring and lifting the mixture only 2–3 times. Do not over-mix.

- Use a spatula to scrape the marshmallow mixture into the prepared tin and gently smooth it out. Swirl the reserved peanut butter through the top of the marshmallow. Stand for 2–3 hours, until set.

- Meanwhile, to make the coating, sift the icing sugar and cornflour together. Dust the top of the marshmallow with some of the coating and turn out onto a clean surface. Dust the bottom with more coating. Use a large knife sprayed with oil to cut the marshmallow into pieces. Toss the pieces in the remaining coating, dusting off the excess.

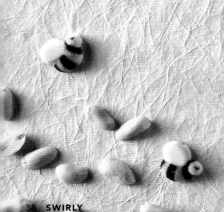

SALTED CARAMEL
&
PEANUT SWIRL

EXHIBIT ONE

Peanut Salted Caramel Swirl Marshmallows

MAKES ABOUT 35

- To make the caramel, combine the sugar, glucose and 60 ml (2 fl oz/¼ cup) water in a medium saucepan over low heat and stir until the sugar dissolves. Brush the sides of the pan with a wet pastry brush to dissolve any crystals that may have formed. Increase the heat to high, bring to the boil and cook, without stirring, until the syrup is golden. Remove from the heat and carefully add the cream. Return to low heat and add the butter 1 piece at a time, whisking until combined. Mix in the salt and peanuts. Leave to cool and thicken.

- Lightly spray a 25 x 30 cm (10 x 12 in) baking tin with oil, line the base and two long sides with non-stick baking paper and lightly spray the paper with oil.

- Prepare the marshmallow mixture – you need to vary the technique slightly, as follows, to give a slightly firmer marshmallow. When the sugar syrup reaches 127°C (260°F), turn off the heat and allow the bubbles to subside. Do not add the gelatine mixture to the sugar syrup. Increase the mixer speed to medium–high and gradually pour the gelatine mixture down the inside of the bowl in a thin, steady stream. Add the hot sugar syrup in the same manner. Continue whisking as instructed, until the mixture is very thick and holds its shape.

- Add a small scoop of marshmallow mixture to the cooled caramel and mix well. Reserve a couple of tablespoons of the caramel and use a large spoon or spatula to gently fold the rest through the marshmallow mixture, stirring and lifting the mixture only 2–3 times. Do not over-mix.

- Use a spatula to scrape the marshmallow mixture into the prepared tin and gently smooth it out. Swirl the reserved caramel through the top of the marshmallow. Stand for 2–3 hours, until set.

- Meanwhile, to make the coating, sift the icing sugar and cornflour together.

- Use the overhanging paper to lift the marshmallow out of the tin. Use a large knife sprayed lightly with oil to cut it into pieces. Gently dust the marshmallow pieces in the coating if you find them too sticky to handle.

1 quantity Classic vanilla marshmallow mixture (page 8)

PEANUT SALTED CARAMEL

220 g (7¾ oz/1 cup) sugar
1 tablespoon glucose syrup
125 ml (4 fl oz/½ cup) cream
50 g (1¾ oz) butter, cubed
¼ teaspoon fine sea salt flakes
160 g (5½ oz/1 cup) salted roasted peanuts, roughly chopped

COATING

30 g (1 oz/¼ cup) icing (confectioners') sugar
30 g (1 oz/¼ cup) cornflour (cornstarch)

NOTES

Keep in an airtight container for 2–3 days.

This delicious marshmallow is a little bit oozy so it requires patience when dusting in the coating, but it's definitely worth the effort!

Serve in paper cases if you like.

Apple, Spice & Chocolate Hazelnut Swirl Marshmallows

MAKES ABOUT 35

- Lightly spray a 25 x 30 cm (10 x 12 in) baking tin with oil, line the base and two long sides with non-stick baking paper and lightly spray the paper with oil. Combine 460 g (1 lb ¼ oz/2 cups) of the sugar, the glucose and 185 ml (6¼ fl oz/¾ cup) water in a small, deep heavy-based saucepan. Stir over low heat until the sugar dissolves. Bring to the boil and simmer, without stirring, until the syrup reaches 127°C (260°F) on a sugar thermometer (this is the upper end of the hard-ball stage).

- Meanwhile, slowly sprinkle the gelatine over 160 ml (5¼ fl oz/⅔ cup) cold water in a shallow microwave-safe bowl and set aside for 5 minutes. Heat in the microwave for 30–45 seconds on High (100%), or until the gelatine has dissolved and the liquid is clear. Watch it carefully, as the syrup has a tendency to bubble up.

- When the sugar syrup reaches 115°C (239°F), whisk the egg whites in an electric mixer with a whisk attachment on medium speed. When frothy, increase the speed to medium–high and gradually add the remaining sugar, whisking until thick and glossy. Keep the mixer running on medium speed. When the sugar syrup reaches 127°C (260°F), turn off the heat. When the bubbles subside, carefully add the dissolved gelatine – take care, as the mixture may bubble up.

- Increase the mixer speed to medium–high and gradually pour the hot syrup mixture down the inside of the bowl in a thin, steady stream. Increase the speed to high and continue whisking until the mixture is thick. Gradually add the spice and apple juice concentrate and whisk until the mixture is very thick and holds its shape, about 10–12 minutes. The outside of the bowl should almost be at room temperature.

- Meanwhile, put the chocolate hazelnut spread in a small microwave-safe bowl. Heat in the microwave on Medium (50%) in 15-second bursts until it is just pourable, but not hot. Reserve 1 tablespoon and use a large spoon or spatula to gently fold the rest through the marshmallow mixture, stirring and lifting the mixture only 2–3 times. Do not over-mix.

- Use a spatula to scrape the marshmallow mixture into the prepared tin and gently smooth it out. Swirl the reserved chocolate hazelnut spread through the top of the marshmallow. Stand for 2–3 hours, until set.

- Meanwhile, to make the coating, sift the icing sugar and cornflour together. Dust the top of the marshmallow with some of the coating and turn out onto a clean surface. Dust the bottom with more coating. Use a large knife or cutters sprayed lightly with oil to cut the marshmallow into pieces. Toss the marshmallow pieces in the remaining coating, dusting off the excess. Serve with hot chocolate if you like.

515 g (1 lb 2½ oz/2¼ cups) caster (superfine) sugar

1 tablespoon glucose syrup

2 tablespoons powdered gelatine

70 g (2½ oz/2 large) egg whites, at room temperature

¼ teaspoon mixed (pumpkin pie) spice

2 tablespoons apple juice concentrate (see Notes)

230 g (8 oz/¾ cup) chocolate hazelnut spread

Hot chocolate to serve, if desired

COATING

30 g (1 oz/¼ cup) icing (confectioners') sugar

30 g (1 oz/¼ cup) cornflour (cornstarch)

NOTES

Keep in an airtight container for 2–3 days.

Apple juice concentrate is available in the health food aisle of most supermarkets.

CUTESY

CHAPTER 4

Chocolate Honeycomb Marshmallows

MAKES ABOUT 48

- Lightly spray a 20 x 30 cm (8 x 12 in) slice tin, the holes of four 12-hole round-based gem irons, 30 ml (1 fl oz) silicon baking moulds or 30 ml (1 fl oz) mini muffin pans with oil. Set aside 2 tablespoons of the sugar. Combine the remaining sugar, the glucose and 125 ml (4 fl oz/½ cup) water in a small, deep heavy-based saucepan. Stir over low heat until the sugar dissolves. Bring to the boil and simmer, without stirring, until the syrup reaches 116°C (241°F) on a sugar thermometer (soft-ball stage). Watch it carefully, as the syrup has a tendency to bubble up.

- Meanwhile, slowly sprinkle the gelatine over 125 ml (4 fl oz/½ cup) cold water in a shallow microwave-safe bowl and set aside for 5 minutes. Heat in the microwave for 30–45 seconds on High (100%), or until gelatine has dissolved.

- When the syrup reaches 110°C (230°F), whisk the egg whites in an electric mixer with a whisk attachment on medium speed. When frothy, increase the speed to medium–high and gradually add the reserved sugar, whisking until thick and glossy. Keep the mixer running on medium speed.

- When the sugar syrup reaches 116°C (241°F), turn off the heat and allow the bubbles to subside.

- Increase the mixer speed to medium–high and gradually pour the gelatine mixture down the inside of the bowl in a thin, steady stream. Add the hot sugar syrup in the same manner. Increase the speed to high and whisk for 5 minutes. Gradually add the golden syrup and continue to whisk until the mixture is very thick and holds its shape, about 8–10 minutes in total, depending on your mixer. The outside of the bowl should almost be at room temperature.

- Use a spatula to scrape the marshmallow mixture into the prepared rectangular pan or scoop the marshmallow mixture into a large piping bag fitted with a 10 mm (½ in) nozzle and pipe into the oiled moulds. (You can spoon the mixture into the moulds if you prefer.) Stand for 1–2 hours, until set.

- Meanwhile, to make the coating, sift the icing sugar and the cornflour together.

- Cut the marshmallow into shapes with a lightly oiled large knife or remove the marshmallows from their moulds. Toss the pieces in the coating, dusting off the excess well. Dunk the marshmallows, one at a time, in the melted chocolate and scoop out with a fork, allowing the excess chocolate to drip off. Place on a tray lined with non-stick baking paper and leave to set.

310 g (11 oz/1⅓ cups) raw caster (superfine) sugar
1 tablespoon glucose syrup
1½ tablespoons powdered gelatine
70 g (2½ oz/2 large) egg whites, at room temperature
115 g (4 oz/⅓ cup) golden syrup
500 g (1 lb 2 oz) dark chocolate, melted

COATING
2 tablespoons icing (confectioners') sugar
2 tablespoons cornflour (cornstarch)

NOTES
Keep in an airtight container for 1–2 days.

Add a few drops of yellow food colouring to highlight the 'honeycomb' colour if you like.

Jam Doughnut Marshmallows

MAKES ABOUT 24

1 quantity Classic vanilla
marshmallow mixture
(page 8)
2 tablespoons raspberry jam

CINNAMON SUGAR COATING
75 g (2½ oz/⅓ cup) sugar
½ teaspoon ground cinnamon

NOTES

*Keep in an airtight container
for 2–3 days.*

*You can spoon the mixture into
the oiled moulds if you like,
though piping is quicker.*

- Lightly spray four 12-hole round-based gem irons, 30 ml (1 fl oz) silicon baking moulds or 30 ml (1 fl oz) mini muffin pans with oil.

- Prepare the marshmallow mixture as instructed.

- Transfer the mixture to 2 large piping bags fitted with plain nozzles and pipe into the oiled moulds, ensuring you do not over-fill them. The top of the marshmallow mixture should be flush with the tops of the holes. Use a teaspoon dunked in very hot water, then dried, to scoop a slight indent in the centre of each marshmallow. This is where the jam will go. Spoon about ⅛ teaspoon of jam into each indent. Stand for 1–2 hours, until set.

- Meanwhile, to make the coating, mix the sugar and cinnamon together.

- Carefully slide 2 marshmallows out of their holes and sandwich together. They should be sticky enough to join together securely. Repeat with the remaining marshmallows, then roll in the coating.

Filled Chocolate Marshmallows

MAKES ABOUT 24

285 g (10 oz/1¼ cups) caster (superfine) sugar

2 teaspoons glucose syrup

5 teaspoons powdered gelatine

85 g (3 oz) chocolate hazelnut spread

35 g (1¼ oz/1 large) egg white, at room temperature

1½ tablespoons Dutch (unsweetened) cocoa powder

40 g (1½ oz) chopped dark chocolate

Whipped cream and cherries to serve, if desired

COCOA COATING

2 tablespoons icing (confectioners') sugar, sifted

1 tablespoon cornflour (cornstarch), sifted

3 teaspoons Dutch (unsweetened) cocoa powder

NOTE

Keep in an airtight container for 2–3 days.

- To make the coating, sift the icing sugar, cornflour and cocoa together. Lightly spray two 12-hole round-based gem irons, 30 ml (1 fl oz) silicon baking moulds, 30 ml (1 fl oz) mini muffin pans with oil and dust with some of the coating. Set aside 2 tablespoons of the sugar.

- Combine the remaining sugar, the glucose and 80 ml (2½ fl oz/⅓ cup) water in a small, deep heavy-based saucepan. Stir over low heat until the sugar dissolves. Bring to the boil and simmer, without stirring, until the syrup reaches 127°C (260°F) on a sugar thermometer (this is the upper end of the hard-ball stage). Watch it carefully, as the syrup has a tendency to bubble up.

- Meanwhile, slowly sprinkle the gelatine over 80 ml (3 fl oz/⅓ cup) cold water in a shallow microwave-safe bowl and set aside for 5 minutes. Heat in the microwave for 30–45 seconds on High (100%), or until the gelatine has dissolved.

- Spoon the chocolate hazelnut spread into a small piping bag fitted with a plain 3 mm (⅛ in) nozzle or a medium snap-lock bag. Set aside.

- When the sugar syrup reaches 115°C (239°F), whisk the egg white in an electric mixer with a whisk attachment on medium speed. When frothy, increase the speed to medium–high and gradually add the reserved sugar, whisking until thick and glossy. Keep the mixer running on medium speed.

- When the sugar syrup reaches 127°C (260°F), turn off the heat. When the bubbles subside, carefully add the dissolved gelatine – take care, as the mixture may bubble up.

- Increase the mixer speed to medium–high and gradually pour the hot syrup mixture down the inside of the bowl in a thin, steady stream. Increase the speed to high and continue to whisk until the mixture is very thick and holds its shape, about 8–10 minutes, depending on your mixer. The outside of the bowl should almost be at room temperature. Sift the cocoa over the top of the marshmallow mixture, add the chocolate and gently fold to combine.

- Spoon the mixture into a large piping bag fitted with a plain 5 mm (¼ in) nozzle and half-fill each prepared mould, covering the base. Pipe about ¼ teaspoon chocolate hazelnut spread into the centre of each, then top up with the remaining marshmallow mixture, enclosing the filling. Stand for 2–3 hours, until set. Remove from the holes or cases and toss the marshmallows in the remaining coating. May be served as an ice-cream sundae if desired.

Gingerbread Marshmallows with Almond Praline

MAKES ABOUT 12

345 g (12 oz/1½ cups) raw caster (superfine) sugar

80 g (2¾ oz/⅓ cup, firmly packed) dark brown sugar

90 g (3¼ oz/¼ cup) golden syrup

2 tablespoons powdered gelatine

70 g (2½ oz/2 large) egg whites, at room temperature

¾ teaspoon ground ginger

ALMOND PRALINE

125 g (4½ oz/1 cup) slivered almonds, toasted

275 g (9¾ oz/1¼ cups) sugar

COATING

2 tablespoons icing (confectioners') sugar, sifted

2 tablespoons cornflour (cornstarch), sifted

NOTES

Keep in an airtight container for 2–3 days (roll in praline just before serving).

This mixture can also be set in a 25 x 30 cm (10 x 12 in) baking tin, lined with non-stick baking paper that is then sprayed with oil. Once set, cut the marshmallow as desired.

This marshmallow is surprisingly light and airy.

- Lightly spray two 20 x 30 cm (8 x 12 in) slice tins with oil, line the base and two long sides with non-stick baking paper and spray the paper with oil. Combine 285 g (10 oz/1¼ cups) of the caster sugar, the dark brown sugar, golden syrup and 185 ml (6¼ fl oz/¾ cup) water in a deep heavy-based saucepan. Stir over low heat until the sugar dissolves. Bring to the boil and simmer, without stirring, until the syrup reaches 112°C (234°F) on a sugar thermometer. Watch it carefully, as the syrup has a tendency to bubble up.

- Meanwhile, slowly sprinkle the gelatine over 185 ml (6¼ fl oz/¾ cup) cold water in a shallow microwave-safe bowl and set aside for 5 minutes. Heat in the microwave for 30–45 seconds on High (100%), or until the gelatine has dissolved.

- When the sugar syrup reaches 108°C (226°F), whisk the egg whites in an electric mixer with a whisk attachment on medium speed. When frothy, increase the speed to medium–high and gradually add the remaining sugar, whisking until thick and glossy. Keep the mixer running on medium speed. When the sugar syrup reaches 112°C (234°F), turn off the heat and allow the bubbles to subside.

- Increase the mixer speed to medium–high and gradually pour the gelatine mixture down the inside of the bowl in a thin, steady stream. Add the hot sugar syrup in the same manner. Increase the speed to high and continue whisking until the mixture is thick. Add the ginger and whisk until the mixture is very thick and holds its shape, about 12–14 minutes, depending on your mixer. The outside of the bowl should almost be at room temperature. Use a spatula to scrape the marshmallow mixture into the prepared tins and smooth the surface of each. Stand for 2–3 hours, until set.

- Meanwhile, to make the almond praline, spread the almonds over a tray lined with non-stick baking paper. Combine the sugar and 60 ml (2 fl oz/¼ cup) water in a small saucepan. Stir over low heat until the sugar dissolves, brushing the sides of the pan with a clean pastry brush dipped in water to dissolve any crystals that may have formed. Bring to the boil and cook, without stirring, until the syrup is golden. Immediately pour over the almonds to cover. Allow to set, then finely chop the praline. Store in an airtight container until required.

- To make the coating, sift the icing sugar and cornflour together. Dust the top of each marshmallow with some of the coating and turn out onto a clean surface. Dust the bottom of each with more coating. Just before serving, use a 9.5 cm (3¾ in) gingerbread-man cutter sprayed with oil to cut the marshmallow into shapes. Roll the sticky sides of each marshmallow in the praline.

Super Artsy Marshmallows

MAKES ABOUT 24

- Lightly spray 3 large trays with oil. To make the coating, sift the icing sugar and cornflour together. Dust some of the coating over the trays.

- Slowly sprinkle the gelatine over 160 ml (5½ fl oz/⅔ cup) cold water in a shallow microwave-safe bowl and set aside for 5 minutes. Heat in the microwave for 30–45 seconds on High (100%) or until the gelatine has dissolved.

- Meanwhile, combine the sugar and 160 ml (5½ fl oz/⅔ cup) water in a medium saucepan and stir over medium heat until the sugar has dissolved. Remove from the heat. Whisk in the dissolved gelatine. Set aside to cool to room temperature, about 30 minutes.

- Pour the mixture into a large bowl and use an electric mixer with a whisk attachment to whisk on high speed until thick. Add the vanilla and continue to whisk until mixture is very thick and holds its shape, about 8–10 minutes, depending on your mixer.

- Dollop spoonfuls of the marshmallow mixture onto the prepared trays. Stand for about 1 hour, until set.

- Sprinkle the marshmallows with decorations. Put a spoonful of the remaining coating in a tea strainer and carefully dust around the edges of the marshmallows so they're not too sticky to handle. If you get any coating on the decorations simply brush it off gently with a soft, dry pastry brush.

NOTES

Keep in an airtight container for 2–3 days.

You can also set the mixture in a 20 x 30 cm (8 x 12 in) slice tin, lined with non-stick baking paper that is then sprayed lightly with oil. Once set, turn out onto a clean surface and use a large knife sprayed lightly with oil to cut the marshmallow into bite-sized pieces. Toss in hundreds and thousands, toasted coconut or even coloured coconut.

2 tablespoons powdered
    gelatine
345 g (12 oz/1½ cups) caster
    (superfine) sugar
2 teaspoons vanilla extract
Coloured sanding sugar
    or hundreds and thousands
    to decorate

COATING
2 tablespoons icing
    (confectioners') sugar
2 tablespoons cornflour
    (cornstarch)

Orange Blossom Marshmallows

MAKES ABOUT 12

- Lightly spray a 25 x 30 cm (10 x 12 in) baking tin with oil, line the base and two long sides with non-stick baking paper and lightly spray the paper with oil.

- Combine 460 g (1 lb ¼ oz/2 cups) of the sugar, the glucose and 185 ml (6¼ fl oz/¾ cup) water in a small, deep heavy-based saucepan. Stir over low heat until the sugar dissolves. Bring to the boil and simmer, without stirring, until the syrup reaches 127°C (260°F) on a sugar thermometer (this is the upper end of the hard-ball stage). Watch it carefully, as the syrup has a tendency to bubble up.

- Meanwhile, slowly sprinkle the gelatine over 185 ml (6¼ fl oz/¾ cup) cold water in a shallow microwave-safe bowl and set aside for 5 minutes. Heat in the microwave for 30–45 seconds on High (100%), or until the gelatine has dissolved and the liquid is clear.

- When the sugar syrup reaches 115°C (239°F), whisk the egg whites in an electric mixer with a whisk attachment on medium speed. When frothy, increase the speed to medium–high and gradually add the remaining sugar, whisking until thick and glossy. Keep the mixer running on medium speed.

- When the sugar syrup reaches 127°C (260°F), turn off the heat. When the bubbles subside, carefully add the dissolved gelatine – take care, as the mixture may bubble up.

- Increase the mixer speed to medium–high and gradually pour the hot syrup mixture down the inside of the bowl in a thin, steady stream. Increase the speed to high and continue whisking until the mixture is thick. Add the orange blossom water and food colouring, and whisk until the mixture is very thick and holds its shape, about 10–12 minutes, depending on your mixer. The outside of the bowl should almost be at room temperature.

- Use a spatula to scrape the marshmallow mixture into the prepared tin and smooth the surface. Stand for 2–3 hours, until set.

- Meanwhile, to make the coating, sift the icing sugar and cornflour together.

- Dust the top of the marshmallow with some of the coating and turn out onto a clean surface. Dust the bottom with more coating. Use a 7.5 cm (3 in) flower-shaped cutter sprayed lightly with oil to cut the marshmallow into shapes. Roll the sticky sides of each marshmallow piece in the decorations and carefully insert lollipop sticks.

515 g (1 lb 2½ oz/2¼ cups) caster (superfine) sugar

1 tablespoon glucose syrup

2 tablespoons powdered gelatine

70 g (2½ oz/2 large) egg whites, at room temperature

½ teaspoon orange blossom water, or to taste (see Notes)

Orange food colouring

Coloured sanding sugar, sprinkles or mini cachous to decorate (see Notes)

12 lollipop sticks (see Notes)

COATING

2 tablespoons icing (confectioners') sugar

2 tablespoons cornflour (cornstarch)

NOTES

Keep in an airtight container for 2–3 days.

Orange blossom water is available from Middle Eastern and gourmet grocery stores. It varies in strength, so be careful not to overdo it. A hint is preferable to over-perfumed.

Sanding sugar, mini cachous and lollipop sticks are available from specialty cake decorating stores or online.

Marbled Chocolate Bunnies

MAKES ABOUT 12

- Lightly spray a 25 x 30 cm (10 x 12 in) baking tin with oil, line the base and two long sides with non-stick baking paper and lightly spray the paper with oil.

- Combine 460 g (1 lb ¼ oz/2 cups) of the sugar, the glucose and 185 ml (6¼ fl oz/¾ cup) water in a small, deep heavy-based saucepan. Stir over low heat until the sugar dissolves. Bring to the boil and simmer, without stirring, until the syrup reaches 127°C (260°F) on a sugar thermometer (this is the upper end of the hard-ball stage). Watch it carefully, as the syrup has a tendency to bubble up.

- Meanwhile, slowly sprinkle the gelatine over 185 ml (6¼ fl oz/¾ cup) cold water in a shallow microwave-safe bowl and set aside for 5 minutes. Heat in the microwave for 30–45 seconds on High (100%), or until the gelatine has dissolved and the liquid is clear.

- When the sugar syrup reaches 115°C (239°F), whisk the egg whites in an electric mixer with a whisk attachment on medium speed. When frothy, increase the speed to medium–high and gradually add the remaining sugar, whisking until thick and glossy. Keep the mixer running on medium speed.

- When the sugar syrup reaches 127°C (260°F), turn off the heat. When the bubbles subside, carefully add the dissolved gelatine – take care, as the mixture may bubble up.

- Increase the mixer speed to medium–high and gradually pour the hot syrup mixture down the inside of the bowl in a thin, steady stream. Increase the speed to high and whisk until the mixture is very thick and holds its shape, about 10–12 minutes, depending on your mixer. The outside of the bowl should almost be at room temperature.

- Transfer half the marshmallow mixture to a separate bowl and use a large spoon or spatula to fold in the dark chocolate. Fold the milk chocolate into the remaining marshmallow, then use a spatula to scrape this into the dark-chocolate mixture. Gently fold the mixtures together 1–2 times, then scrape into the prepared tin and smooth the surface. Stand for 2–3 hours, until set.

- Turn the marshmallow out onto a clean surface. Use bunny-shaped cutters sprayed lightly with oil to cut the marshmallow into shapes. Roll the bunnies in the coconut to cover completely.

515 g (1 lb 2½ oz/2¼ cups) caster (superfine) sugar
1 tablespoon glucose syrup
2 tablespoons powdered gelatine
70 g (2½ oz/2 large) egg whites, at room temperature
50 g (1¾ oz) dark chocolate, melted and cooled
50 g (1¾ oz) milk chocolate, melted and cooled
90 g (3¼ oz/1½ cups) shredded coconut

NOTES

Keep in an airtight container for 2–3 days.

You will lose some volume when you add the chocolate, giving these marshmallows a slightly more dense texture.

Marshmallow Sherbet Cones

24 medium ice-cream cup
    cones (see Notes)
1 quantity Super artsy
    marshmallow mixture
    (page 55)
Hundreds and thousands
    or sprinkles to decorate

SHERBET
60 g (2¼ oz/½ cup)
    icing (confectioners')
    sugar
2 teaspoons citric acid

- To make the sherbet, sift the icing sugar and citric acid together. Place a teaspoon of sherbet in the base of each cup cone.

- Prepare the marshmallow mixture as instructed and immediately transfer to a large piping bag fitted with a medium star nozzle. Fill the cup cones with swirls of marshmallow and decorate with sprinkles. Stand for about an hour, until set.

NOTES

These are best eaten on the day they are made.

Ice-cream cup cones are flat-bottomed cones, available from supermarkets.

If you are feeling creative, colour the marshmallow with food colouring and add different flavoured oils. Try green and peppermint, or pink and raspberry.

For an extra special treat, coat the insides of the cones with melted chocolate!

Honeyed Cardamom Marshmallows with Pistachios

MAKES ABOUT 35 LARGE OR DOZENS OF SMALL

- Lightly spray 3–4 large trays or a 25 x 30 cm (10 x 12 in) baking tin with oil. Line the base and two long sides of the tin with non-stick baking paper and lightly spray the paper with oil, if using.

- Combine 345 g (12 oz/1½ cups) of the sugar, the honey and 125 ml (4 fl oz/½ cup) water in a medium, deep heavy-based saucepan. Stir over low heat until the sugar dissolves. Bring to the boil and simmer, without stirring, until the syrup reaches 127°C (260°F) on a sugar thermometer (this is the upper end of the hard-ball stage). Watch it carefully, as the syrup has a tendency to bubble up.

- Meanwhile, slowly sprinkle the gelatine over 160 ml (5¼ fl oz/⅔ cup) in a microwave-safe bowl and set aside for 5 minutes. Heat in the microwave for 30–45 seconds on High (100%), or until the gelatine has dissolved.

- When the sugar syrup reaches 115°C (239°F), whisk the egg whites in an electric mixer with a whisk attachment on medium speed. When frothy, increase the speed to medium–high and gradually add the remaining sugar, whisking until thick and glossy. Keep the mixer running on medium speed.

- When the sugar syrup reaches 127°C (260°F), turn off the heat and allow the bubbles to subside.

- Increase the mixer speed to medium–high and gradually pour the gelatine mixture down the inside of the bowl in a thin, steady stream. Add the hot sugar syrup in the same manner. Increase the speed to high and continue whisking until the mixture is thick. Add the cardamom and whisk until the mixture is very thick and holds its shape, about 10–12 minutes, depending on your mixer. The outside of the bowl should almost be at room temperature.

- Use a spatula to scrape the marshmallow mixture into a large piping bag fitted with a plain 5 mm (¼ in) nozzle and pipe small marshmallows onto prepared trays, or scrape into the prepared tin and smooth the surface. Stand for 2–3 hours, until set.

- Meanwhile, to make the coating, sift the icing sugar and cornflour together.

- Toss half of the small marshmallows in the coating mixture and half in the pistachios. For the marshmallow made in the tin, dust the top with some of the coating and turn out onto a clean surface. Dust the bottom with more coating, dusting off the excess. Use a large knife sprayed lightly with oil to cut the marshmallow into bite-sized pieces. Roll the sticky sides of each piece of marshmallow in the chopped nuts.

400 g (14 oz/1¾ cups) caster (superfine) sugar
150 g (5½ oz) honey
2 tablespoons powdered gelatine
70 g (2½ oz/2 large) egg whites, at room temperature
¼ teaspoon ground cardamom
110 g (3¾ oz/¾ cup) shelled pistachio nuts, lightly toasted, chopped

COATING

2 tablespoons icing (confectioners') sugar
2 tablespoons cornflour (cornstarch)

NOTE

Keep in an airtight container for 2–3 days.

CHAPTER 5

BOOZY

B52 Marshmallows

MAKES ABOUT 30

515 g (1 lb 2½ oz/2¼ cups) caster (superfine) sugar

1 tablespoon glucose syrup

2 tablespoons powdered gelatine

1 teaspoon instant coffee granules

70 g (2½ oz/2 large) egg whites, at room temperature

1 tablespoon Kahlua liqueur

1 tablespoon Baileys liqueur

1 tablespoon Cointreau liqueur

Orange food colouring

COATING

30 g (1 oz/¼ cup) icing (confectioners') sugar

30 g (1 oz/¼ cup) cornflour (cornstarch)

NOTES

These marshmallows are best eaten on the day they are made.

You will lose some volume when you add the liqueurs, giving these marshmallows a slightly denser texture.

- Lightly spray a 20 x 30 cm (8 x 12 in) slice tin with oil, line the base and two long sides with non-stick baking paper and lightly spray the paper with oil.

- Combine 460 g (1 lb ¼ oz/2 cups) of the sugar, the glucose and 185 ml (6¼ fl oz/¾ cup) water in a small, deep heavy-based saucepan. Stir over low heat until the sugar dissolves. Bring to the boil and simmer, without stirring, until the syrup reaches 121°C (250°F) on a sugar thermometer (hard-ball stage). Watch it carefully, as the syrup has a tendency to bubble up.

- Meanwhile, slowly sprinkle the gelatine over 160 ml (5¼ fl oz/⅔ cup) cold water in a shallow microwave-safe bowl and set aside for 5 minutes. Heat in the microwave for 30–45 seconds on High (100%), or until the gelatine has dissolved and the liquid is clear. Dissolve the coffee granules in 1 teaspoon hot water and set aside.

- When the sugar syrup reaches 112°C (234°F), whisk the egg whites in an electric mixer with a whisk attachment on medium speed. When frothy, increase the speed to medium–high and gradually add the remaining sugar, whisking until thick and glossy. Keep the mixer running on medium speed.

- When the sugar syrup reaches 121°C (250°F), turn off the heat. When the bubbles subside, carefully add the dissolved gelatine – take care, as the mixture may bubble up.

- Increase the mixer speed to medium–high and gradually pour the hot syrup mixture down the inside of the bowl in a thin, steady stream. Increase the speed to high and continue whisking until the mixture is very thick and holds its shape, about 10–12 minutes, depending on your mixer. The outside of the bowl should almost be at room temperature.

- Divide the marshmallow mixture into three portions and, working quickly, fold the Kahlua and coffee into one portion with a large spoon or spatula. Spoon into the prepared tin. Fold the Baileys into another portion and carefully spoon it evenly over the Kahlua marshmallow. Finally, fold the Cointreau and a few drops of orange food colouring into the remaining portion and pour evenly over the Baileys marshmallow. Stand for 2–3 hours, until set.

- Meanwhile, to make the coating, sift the icing sugar and cornflour together.

- Dust the top of the marshmallow with some of the coating and turn out onto a clean surface. Dust the bottom with more coating. Use a 6 cm (2½ in) rocket-shaped cutter sprayed lightly with oil to cut the marshmallow into shapes. Toss the marshmallow pieces in the remaining coating, dusting off the excess.

Cointreau & Honey Marshmallows with Pine Nut Praline

MAKES ABOUT 30

- Lightly spray a 25 x 30 cm (10 x 12 in) baking tin with oil, line the base and two long sides with non-stick baking paper and spray with oil. Combine 345 g (12 oz/1½ cups) of the sugar, the honey and 125 ml (4 fl oz/½ cup) water in a deep, heavy-based saucepan. Stir over low heat until the sugar dissolves. Bring to the boil and simmer, without stirring, until the syrup reaches 127°C (260°F) on a sugar thermometer (this is the upper end of the hard-ball stage). Watch carefully, as the syrup has a tendency to bubble up.

- Meanwhile, slowly sprinkle the gelatine over 160 ml (5¼ fl oz/⅔ cup) cold water in a shallow microwave-safe bowl and set aside for 5 minutes. Heat in the microwave for 30–45 seconds on High (100%), or until the gelatine has dissolved.

- When the sugar syrup reaches 115°C (239°F), whisk the egg whites in an electric mixer with a whisk attachment on medium speed. When frothy, increase the speed to medium–high and gradually add the remaining sugar, whisking until thick and glossy. Keep the mixer running on medium speed. When the sugar syrup reaches 127°C (260°F), turn off the heat and allow the bubbles to subside.

- Increase the mixer speed to medium–high and gradually pour the gelatine mixture down the inside of the bowl in a thin, steady stream. Add the hot sugar syrup in the same manner. Increase the speed to high and whisk for 5 minutes. Add the Cointreau and whisk until the mixture is very thick and holds its shape, about 12–15 minutes, depending on your mixer. The outside of the bowl should almost be at room temperature. Use a spatula to scrape the marshmallow mixture into the prepared tin and smooth the surface. Stand for 2–3 hours, until set.

- Meanwhile, to make the coating, sift the icing sugar and cornflour together.

- To make the pine nut praline, spread the pine nuts over a tray lined with non-stick baking paper. Combine the sugar and 60 ml (2 fl oz/¼ cup) water in a small saucepan. Stir over low heat until the sugar dissolves, brushing the sides of the pan with a clean pastry brush dipped in water to dissolve any crystals that may have formed. Bring to the boil and cook, without stirring, until the syrup is golden. Immediately pour over the pine nuts to cover. Allow to set, then finely chop the praline. Store in an airtight container until required.

- Dust the top of the marshmallow with some of the coating and turn out onto a clean surface. Dust the bottom with more coating, dusting off the excess. Use a 5 cm (2 in) heart-shaped cutter sprayed lightly with oil to cut the marshmallow into shapes. Just before serving, roll the sticky sides of each marshmallow in the praline.

---

400 g (14 oz/1¾ cups) caster (superfine) sugar

150 g (5½ oz) honey

2 tablespoons powdered gelatine

70 g (2½ oz/2 large) egg whites, at room temperature

2 tablespoons Cointreau liqueur

PINE NUT PRALINE

80 g (2¾ oz/½ cup) pine nuts, toasted

110 g (3¾ oz/½ cup) sugar

COATING

2 tablespoons icing (confectioners') sugar

2 tablespoons cornflour (cornstarch)

NOTES

Keep in an airtight container for 1–2 days (coat in praline just before serving).

Add a few drops of orange food colouring if you like.

These are also lovely when made in large heart-shaped silicon moulds. Serve sprinkled with praline.

Cranberry Cosmopolitan Marshmallows

MAKES ABOUT 48 SMALL, OR 6 LARGE

515 g (1 lb 2½ oz/2¼ cups) caster (superfine) sugar

1 tablespoon glucose syrup

360 ml (12½ fl oz) cranberry juice

2 tablespoons powdered gelatine

70 g (2½ oz/2 large) egg whites, at room temperature

60 ml (2 fl oz/¼ cup) vodka

½ teaspoon finely grated orange zest

CRANBERRY COATING

140 g (5 oz/⅔ cup) raw (demerara) sugar

75 g (2½ oz/½ cup) sweetened dried cranberries, finely chopped

NOTES

Keep in an airtight container for 2–3 days.

Add a few drops of pink food colouring if you would like to intensify the 'cranberry' colour.

- Lightly spray a 20 x 30 cm (8 x 12 in) slice tin with oil, line the base and two long sides with non-stick baking paper and lightly spray the paper with oil.

- Combine 460 g (1 lb ¼ oz/2 cups) of the sugar, the glucose and 185 ml (6¼ fl oz/¾ cup) of the juice in a small, deep heavy-based saucepan. Stir over low heat until the sugar dissolves. Bring to the boil and simmer, without stirring, until the syrup reaches 127°C (260°F) on a sugar thermometer (this is the upper end of the hard-ball stage). Watch it carefully, as the syrup has a tendency to bubble up.

- Meanwhile, slowly sprinkle the gelatine over the remaining cranberry juice in a shallow microwave-safe bowl and set aside for 5 minutes. Heat in the microwave for 30–45 seconds on High (100%), or until the gelatine has dissolved.

- When the sugar syrup reaches 115°C (239°F), whisk the egg whites in an electric mixer with a whisk attachment on medium speed. When frothy, increase the speed to medium–high and gradually add the remaining sugar, whisking until thick and glossy. Keep the mixer running on medium speed.

- When the sugar syrup reaches 127°C (260°F), turn off the heat and allow the bubbles to subside.

- Increase the mixer speed to medium–high and gradually pour the gelatine mixture down the inside of the bowl in a thin, steady stream. Add the hot sugar syrup in the same manner. Increase the speed to high and continue whisking until the mixture is very thick and holds its shape, about 10–12 minutes, depending on your mixer. The outside of the bowl should almost be at room temperature. Add the vodka and orange zest, being careful to avoid splashing, and whisk until combined.

- Use a spatula to scrape the marshmallow mixture into the prepared tin. Stand for 2–3 hours, until set.

- Meanwhile, to make the cranberry coating, combine the raw sugar and cranberries.

- Turn the marshmallow out onto a clean surface. Use a large knife or cocktail glass-shaped cutter sprayed lightly with oil to cut the marshmallow into bite-sized pieces. Toss the marshmallow pieces in the cranberry coating.

Gin with a Lemon Twist Marshmallows

MAKES ABOUT 24

- Lightly spray a 20 x 30 cm (8 x 12 in) slice tin with oil, line the base and two long sides with non-stick baking paper and lightly spray the paper with oil.

- Combine 460 g (1 lb ¼ oz/2 cups) of the sugar, the glucose and 185 ml (6¼ fl oz/¾ cup) water in a small, deep heavy-based saucepan. Stir over low heat until the sugar dissolves. Bring to the boil and simmer, without stirring, until the syrup reaches 127°C (260°F) on a sugar thermometer (this is the upper end of the hard-ball stage). Watch it carefully, as the syrup has a tendency to bubble up.

- Meanwhile, slowly sprinkle the gelatine over 185 ml (6¼ fl oz/¾ cup) cold water in a shallow microwave-safe bowl and set aside for 5 minutes. Heat in the microwave for 30–45 seconds on High (100%), or until the gelatine has dissolved and the liquid is clear.

- When the sugar syrup reaches 115°C (239°F), whisk the egg whites in an electric mixer with a whisk attachment on medium speed. When frothy, increase the speed to medium–high and gradually add the remaining sugar, whisking until thick and glossy. Keep the mixer running on medium speed.

- When the sugar syrup reaches 127°C (260°F), turn off the heat. When the bubbles subside, carefully add the dissolved gelatine – take care, as the mixture may bubble up.

- Increase the mixer speed to medium–high and gradually pour the hot syrup mixture down the inside of the bowl in a thin, steady stream. Increase the speed to high and continue whisking until the mixture is very thick and holds its shape, about 10–12 minutes, depending on your mixer. The outside of the bowl should almost be at room temperature. Add the gin and lemon zest, being careful to avoid splashing, and whisk until combined.

- Use a spatula to scrape the marshmallow mixture into the prepared tin and smooth the surface. Stand for 2–3 hours, until set.

- Meanwhile, to make the coating, sift the icing sugar and cornflour together. To make the sherbet, sift the icing sugar and citric acid together.

- Dust the top of the marshmallow with some of the coating and turn out onto a clean surface. Dust the bottom with more coating, dusting off the excess. Use a 3.5 cm (1¼ in) cutter sprayed lightly with oil to cut the marshmallow into rounds. Do not coat the sides of the marshmallows. Serve with the sherbet mixture.

515 g (1 lb 2½ oz/2¼ cups) caster (superfine) sugar
1 tablespoon glucose syrup
2 tablespoons powdered gelatine
70 g (2½ oz/2 large) egg whites, at room temperature
1½ tablespoons gin
1 teaspoon finely grated lemon zest

COATING

2 tablespoons icing (confectioners') sugar
2 tablespoons cornflour (cornstarch)

SHERBET

30 g (1 oz/¼ cup) icing (confectioners') sugar
1 teaspoon citric acid

NOTES

May be stored in an airtight container for 2–3 days.

For extra zing, try serving a bowl of popping candy (available from specialty candy stores and online) alongside the sherbet. Sprinkle the candy over the sticky sides of the marshmallows just before you eat them.

Mojito Marshmallows

MAKES ABOUT 26

- Lightly spray a 25 x 30 cm (10 x 12 in) baking tin with oil, line the base and two long sides with non-stick baking paper and lightly spray the paper with oil.

- Combine 460 g (1 lb ¼ oz/2 cups) of the sugar, the glucose and 185 ml (6¼ fl oz/¾ cup) water in a small, deep heavy-based saucepan. Stir over low heat until the sugar dissolves. Add the mint leaves. Bring to the boil and simmer, without stirring, until the syrup reaches 127°C (260°F) on a sugar thermometer (this is the upper end of the hard-ball stage). Watch it carefully, as the syrup has a tendency to bubble up.

- Meanwhile, slowly sprinkle the gelatine over 160 ml (5¼ fl oz/⅔ cup) cold water in a shallow microwave-safe bowl and set aside for 5 minutes. Heat in the microwave for 30–45 seconds on High (100%), or until the gelatine has dissolved and the liquid is clear.

- When the sugar syrup reaches 115°C (239°F), whisk the egg whites in an electric mixer with a whisk attachment on medium speed. When frothy, increase the speed to medium–high and gradually add the remaining sugar, whisking until thick and glossy. Keep the mixer running on medium speed.

- When the sugar syrup reaches 127°C (260°F), turn off the heat and allow the bubbles to subside. Remove the mint leaves with a fork and discard. Carefully add the dissolved gelatine to the syrup – take care, as the mixture may bubble up.

- Increase the mixer speed to medium–high and gradually pour the hot syrup mixture down the inside of the bowl in a thin, steady stream. Increase the speed to high and continue whisking until the mixture is very thick and holds its shape, about 10–12 minutes, depending on your mixer. The outside of the bowl should almost be at room temperature. Add the rum and lime zest, being careful to avoid splashing, and whisk until combined.

- Use a spatula to scrape the marshmallow mixture into the prepared tin and smooth the surface. Stand for 2–3 hours, until set.

- Meanwhile, to make the mint sugar, preheat the oven to 110°C (230°F) and line a tray with non-stick baking paper. Put the sugar and mint in a small food processor and pulse briefly, until just combined. Do not over-process. Spread over the lined tray and cook for 12–15 minutes, or until dry. Remove from the oven and set aside to cool. Crumble the sugar mix if clumps have formed.

- Turn the marshmallow out onto a clean surface. Use a 7 cm (2¾ in) leaf-shaped cutter, or the tip of a small sharp knife sprayed lightly with oil to cut the marshmallow into leaf shapes. Roll the sticky sides of each marshmallow in the mint sugar to coat.

515 g (1 lb 2½ oz/2¼ cups) caster (superfine) sugar

1 tablespoon glucose syrup

1 tablespoon, firmly packed, mint leaves, bruised

2 tablespoons powdered gelatine

70 g (2½ oz/2 large) egg whites, at room temperature

50 ml (1¾ fl oz) white rum

1 teaspoon finely grated lime zest

MINT SUGAR

165 g (5¾ oz/¾ cup) raw (demerara) sugar

¼ cup, firmly packed, mint leaves

NOTE

Keep in an airtight container for 2–3 days.

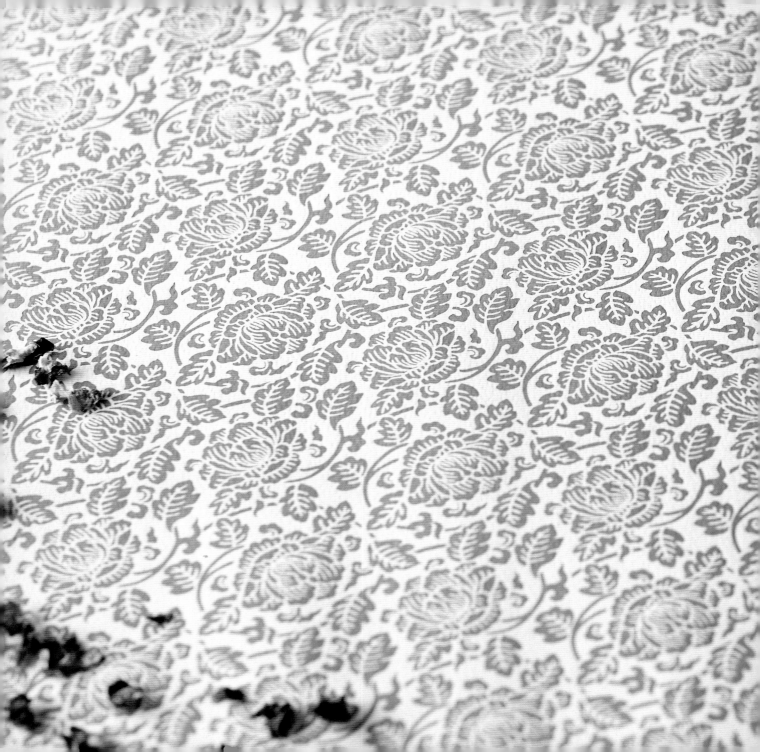

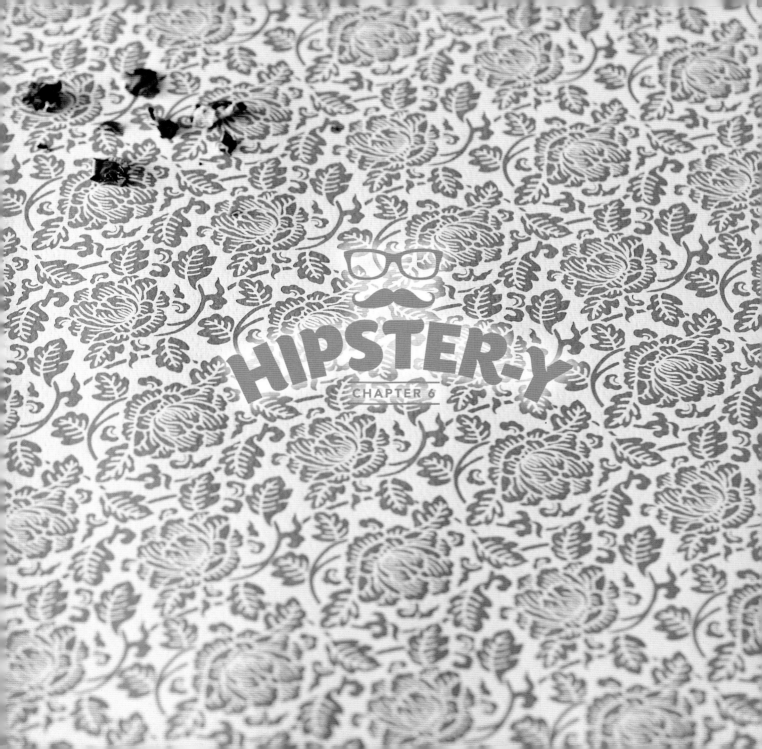

HIPSTER-y

CHAPTER 6

Chai Marshmallows

MAKES ABOUT 30

185 ml (6¼ fl oz/¾ cup) milk
3 chai tea bags
515 g (1 lb 2½ oz/2¼ cups)
   caster (superfine) sugar
1 tablespoon glucose syrup
2 tablespoons powdered
   gelatine
70 g (2½ oz/2 large) egg
   whites, at room temperature

SPICE SUGAR COATING

75 g (2½ oz/⅓ cup) sugar
½ teaspoon ground cinnamon
½ teaspoon ground ginger
½ teaspoon ground star anise

NOTE

*Keep in an airtight container
for 2–3 days.*

*For this picture, we piped the
marshmallow mixture into long
lines with a plain 5 mm (¼ in)
nozzle. Once set, it was cut into
small lengths and tossed in the
spice coating.*

- Lightly spray a 20 x 30 cm (8 x 12 in) slice tin with oil, line the base and two long sides with non-stick baking paper and lightly spray the paper with oil. Bring the milk to a simmer in a small saucepan, add the tea bags and infuse for 5 minutes to make a strong tea. Cool slightly.

- Combine 460 g (1 lb ¼ oz/2 cups) of the sugar, the glucose and 185 ml (6¼ fl oz/¾ cup) water in a small, deep heavy-based saucepan. Stir over low heat until the sugar dissolves. Bring to the boil and simmer, without stirring, until the syrup reaches 127°C (260°F) on a sugar thermometer (this is the upper end of the hard-ball stage). Watch it carefully, as the syrup has a tendency to bubble up.

- Meanwhile, pour the chai into a shallow microwave-safe bowl, slowly whisk in the gelatine and set aside for 5 minutes. Heat in the microwave for 30–45 seconds on High (100%), or until the gelatine has dissolved.

- When the sugar syrup reaches 115°C (239°F), whisk the egg whites in an electric mixer with a whisk attachment on medium speed. When frothy, increase the speed to medium–high and gradually add the remaining sugar, whisking until thick and glossy. Keep the mixer running on medium speed.

- When the sugar syrup reaches 127°C (260°F), turn off the heat and allow the bubbles to subside.

- Increase the mixer speed to medium–high and gradually pour the gelatine mixture down the inside of the bowl in a thin, steady stream. Add the hot sugar syrup in the same manner. Increase the speed to high and whisk until the mixture is very thick and holds its shape, about 6–8 minutes, depending on your mixer. The outside of the bowl should almost be at room temperature.

- Use a spatula to scrape the marshmallow mixture into the prepared tin and smooth the surface. Stand for 2–3 hours, until set.

- Meanwhile, to make the spice sugar coating, mix the sugar and spices together.

- Dust the top of the marshmallow with some of the coating and turn out onto a clean surface. Dust the bottom with more coating. Use a large knife sprayed lightly with oil to cut the marshmallow into 15 squares, then cut each square into two triangles. Toss the marshmallow pieces in the remaining coating, dusting off excess.

Chocolate & Chilli Marshmallows

MAKES ABOUT 35 MEDIUM OR 24 POPS

515 g (1 lb 2½ oz/2¼ cups) caster (superfine) sugar

1 tablespoon glucose syrup

1 small red chilli

2 tablespoons powdered gelatine

70 g (2½ oz/2 large) egg whites, at room temperature

30 g (1 oz/¼ cup) Dutch (unsweetened) cocoa powder

75 g (2½ oz) chopped dark chocolate

24 lollipop sticks

COATING

30 g (1 oz/¼ cup) icing (confectioners') sugar

1½ tablespoons cornflour (cornstarch)

1 tablespoon Dutch (unsweetened) cocoa powder

110 g (3¾ oz/½ cup) raw (demerara) sugar

1 teaspoon dried chilli flakes

NOTES

Keep in an airtight container for 2–3 days.

To add contrast, roll some of the marshmallows in red sanding sugar.

- Lightly spray four 12-hole gem irons, 30 ml (1 fl oz) silicon baking moulds or a 20 x 30 cm (8 x 12 in) slice tin with oil. Line the base and two long sides of the rectangular tin with non-stick baking paper and spray with oil. Combine 460 g (1 lb ¼ oz/2 cups) of the sugar, the glucose and 185 ml (6¼ fl oz/¾ cup) water in a deep heavy-based saucepan. Stir over low heat until the sugar dissolves. Make lengthwise cuts in the chilli, leaving the stem intact, and scrape out the seeds. Add to the syrup, then bring to the boil and simmer, without stirring, until the syrup reaches 127°C (260°F) on a sugar thermometer (this is the upper end of the hard-ball stage). Watch it carefully.

- Meanwhile, slowly sprinkle the gelatine over 185 ml (6¼ fl oz/¾ cup) cold water in a shallow microwave-safe bowl and set aside for 5 minutes. Heat in the microwave for 30–45 seconds on High (100%), or until the gelatine has dissolved.

- When the sugar syrup reaches 115°C (239°F), whisk the egg whites in a mixer with a whisk attachment on medium speed. When frothy, increase the speed to medium–high and gradually add the remaining sugar, whisking until thick and glossy. Keep the mixer running on medium speed. When the sugar syrup reaches 127°C (260°F), turn off the heat and allow the bubbles to subside. Remove the chilli and discard. Carefully add the dissolved gelatine to the syrup – take care, as the mixture may bubble up.

- Increase the mixer speed to medium–high and gradually pour the hot syrup mixture down the inside of the bowl in a thin, steady stream. Increase the speed to high and continue whisking until the mixture is very thick and holds its shape, about 10–12 minutes, depending on your mixer. The outside of the bowl should almost be at room temperature. Sift the cocoa over the top of the marshmallow mixture, add the chocolate and gently fold to combine.

- Pipe or spoon the marshmallow mixture into the oiled moulds, ensuring the surface of each is flat. Or if using the rectangular tin, use a spatula to scrape the marshmallow mixture into the prepared tin and smooth the surface. Stand for 2–3 hours, until set.

- To make the coating, sift the icing sugar, cornflour and cocoa together. In a separate bowl, combine the raw sugar and chilli flakes.

- For the moulded marshmallows, slide 2 out of their moulds and sandwich together. Repeat with the remaining marshmallows. Toss half in the cocoa mixture and half in the chilli flake mixture. Insert the lollipop sticks. For the rectangular marshmallow, dust the top and bottom with the cocoa mixture and cut the marshmallow into bite-sized pieces. Roll the sticky sides of each marshmallow piece in the chilli flake mixture.

Liquorice Marshmallow Twists

MAKES ABOUT 20 TWISTED ROPES

125 ml (4 fl oz/½ cup)
  reduced-fat milk
40 g (1½ oz) soft liquorice,
  roughly chopped
345 g (12 oz/1½ cups) caster
  (superfine) sugar
1 tablespoon glucose syrup
1 tablespoon powdered
  gelatine
35 g (1¼ oz/1 large) egg
  white, at room temperature
½ teaspoon black gel-based
  food colouring (see Notes)

COATING

2 tablespoons icing
  (confectioners') sugar
2 tablespoons cornflour
  (cornstarch)

NOTES

*Keep in an airtight container
for 2–3 days.*

*Gel-based food colouring is
available from cake decorating
stores and some specialty/
gourmet stores, or online.*

*You can also try plaiting the
lengths of marshmallow, or
curling them up in scroll shapes.*

*This technique can be used to
make twists of different colours
and flavours. Use the Citrus
marshmallow from the roulade
recipe (page 102), as it has the
right consistency.*

- Lightly spray 3–4 large trays with oil. Warm the milk and liquorice in a saucepan over low heat, without boiling and stirring often, until the liquorice is soft Blend until smooth, then strain through a fine sieve into a shallow, microwave-safe bowl. Set aside to cool. Set aside 2 tablespoons of the sugar.

- Combine the remaining sugar, the glucose and 125 ml (4 fl oz/½ cup) water in a deep heavy-based saucepan and stir over low heat until the sugar dissolves. Bring to the boil and simmer, without stirring, until the syrup reaches 127°C (260°F) on a sugar thermometer (this is the upper end of the hard-ball stage). Watch it carefully, as the syrup has a tendency to bubble up.

- Meanwhile, slowly sprinkle the gelatine over the liquorice-flavoured milk and whisk to combine. Set aside for 5 minutes. Heat in the microwave for 30–45 seconds on High (100%), or until the gelatine has dissolved.

- When the sugar syrup reaches 115°C (239°F), whisk the egg white in an electric mixer with a whisk attachment on medium speed. When frothy, increase the speed to medium–high and gradually add the reserved sugar, whisking until thick and glossy. Keep the mixer running on medium speed. When the sugar syrup reaches 127°C (260°F), turn off heat and allow the bubbles to subside.

- Increase the mixer speed to medium–high and gradually pour the gelatine mixture down the inside of the bowl in a thin, steady stream. Add the hot sugar syrup in the same manner. Increase the speed to high and whisk until the mixture is very thick and holds its shape, about 8–10 minutes, depending on your mixer. The outside of the bowl should almost be at room temperature. Add the black gel colouring and mix until combined.

- Scoop the marshmallow mixture into a large piping bag fitted with a plain 5 mm (¼ in) nozzle and pipe long parallel lines of marshmallow onto the trays. Stand for about 1 hour, until they are set enough to hold their shape without breaking.

- Meanwhile, to make the coating, sift the icing sugar and cornflour together. Dust your fingers with the coating to stop the marshmallow sticking to them and lay 2 lengths of marshmallow side by side. Place a third length of marshmallow on top. Carefully twist the marshmallow, holding down one end with a flat-bladed knife. Once twisted, weight the other end with another knife. This will stop them unravelling. (Alternatively, once twisted, bring the two ends together and let the ropes intertwine to make a thick double twist.) Repeat with the remaining lengths of marshmallow. Dust lightly with the coating and leave to set for 1–2 hours. Trim the ends and cut into smaller pieces with kitchen scissors.

Coconut, Lemongrass & Palm Sugar Marshmallow Muffins

1 lemongrass stalk

10 kaffir lime leaves

460 g (1 lb ¼ oz/2 cups) raw caster (superfine) sugar

45g (1¾ oz/¼ cup) shaved palm sugar (jaggery)

1 tablespoon glucose syrup

125 ml (4 fl oz/½ cup) coconut milk

2 tablespoons powdered gelatine

70 g (2½ oz/2 large) egg whites, at room temperature

⅛ teaspoon kaffir lime or lime zest

60 g (2¼ oz/1 cup) shredded coconut, toasted

COATING

2 tablespoons icing (confectioners') sugar

2 tablespoons cornflour (cornstarch)

NOTES

Keep in an airtight container for 2–3 days.

If you find you have some marshmallow mixture left over, simply spoon little mounds onto a baking tray lined with non-stick baking paper and sprayed lightly with oil.

- To make the coating, sift the icing sugar and cornflour together. Lightly spray thirty-six 30 ml (1 fl oz) mini muffin holes with oil and dust with the coating. Or, line with mini muffin cases.

- Bruise the lemongrass and 4 of the kaffir lime leaves and put in a small saucepan with 250 ml (8½ fl oz/1 cup) water. Slowly bring to the boil, then turn off the heat. Set aside to cool and for the flavours to infuse. Discard the lemongrass and leaves.

- Combine 400 g (14 oz/1¾ cups) of the caster sugar, the palm sugar, glucose and 185 ml (6¼ fl oz/¾ cup) of the infused water in a small, deep heavy-based saucepan. Stir over low heat until the sugar dissolves. Bring to the boil and simmer, without stirring, until the syrup reaches 121°C (250°F) on a sugar thermometer (hard-ball stage). Watch it carefully, as the syrup has a tendency to bubble up.

- Meanwhile, pour the coconut milk and the remaining infused water into a microwave-safe bowl and add enough water to make 160 ml (5¼ fl oz/⅔ cup). Slowly sprinkle the gelatine over the mixture and set aside for 5 minutes. Heat in the microwave for 30–45 seconds on High (100%), or until the gelatine has dissolved.

- When the sugar syrup reaches 112°C (234°F), whisk the egg whites in an electric mixer with a whisk attachment on medium speed. When frothy, increase the speed to medium–high and gradually add the remaining caster sugar, whisking until thick and glossy. Keep the mixer running on medium speed.

- When the sugar syrup reaches 121°C (250°F), turn off the heat. When the bubbles subside, carefully add the dissolved gelatine – take care, as the mixture may bubble up.

- Increase the mixer speed to medium–high and gradually pour the hot syrup mixture down the inside of the bowl in a thin, steady stream. Add the zest. Increase the speed to high and whisk until the mixture is very thick and holds its shape, about 8–10 minutes, depending on your mixer. The outside of the bowl should almost be at room temperature.

- Spoon or pipe the marshmallow mixture into the prepared muffin holes or cases. Stand for 1–2 hours, until set. Finely shred the remaining kaffir lime leaves and combine with the shredded coconut. Sprinkle over the marshmallows.

Holiday Five-spice Marshmallows

MAKES ABOUT 40

- Lightly spray a 25 x 30 cm (10 x 12 in) baking tin with oil, line the base and two long sides with non-stick baking paper and lightly spray the paper with oil.

- Combine 460 g (1 lb ¼ oz/2 cups) of the sugar, the glucose and 185 ml (6¼ fl oz/¾ cup) water in a small, deep heavy-based saucepan. Stir over low heat until the sugar dissolves. Bring to the boil and simmer, without stirring, until the syrup reaches 127°C (260°F) on a sugar thermometer (this is the upper end of the hard-ball stage). Watch it carefully, as the syrup has a tendency to bubble up.

- Meanwhile, slowly sprinkle the gelatine over 160 ml (5¼ fl oz/⅔ cup) cold water in a shallow microwave-safe bowl and set aside for 5 minutes. Heat in the microwave for 30–45 seconds on High (100%), or until the gelatine has dissolved and the liquid is clear.

- When the sugar syrup reaches 115°C (239°F), whisk the egg whites in an electric mixer with a whisk attachment on medium speed. When frothy, increase the speed to medium–high and gradually add the remaining sugar, whisking until thick and glossy. Keep the mixer running on medium speed.

- When the sugar syrup reaches 127°C (260°F), turn off the heat. When the bubbles subside, carefully add the dissolved gelatine – take care, as the mixture may bubble up.

- Increase the mixer speed to medium–high and gradually pour the hot syrup mixture down the inside of the bowl in a thin, steady stream. Increase the speed to high and continue whisking until the mixture is thick. Slowly add the apple juice concentrate and five-spice, and whisk until the mixture is very thick and holds its shape, about 10–12 minutes, depending on your mixer. The outside of the bowl should almost be at room temperature.

- Use a spatula to scrape the marshmallow mixture into the prepared tin and smooth the surface. Stand for 2–3 hours, until set.

- Use the overhanging baking paper to lift the marshmallow out of the tin. Use cutters sprayed lightly with oil to cut the marshmallow into Christmas shapes. Roll in the coloured sugar to decorate.

515 g (1 lb 2½ oz/2¼ cups) caster (superfine) sugar
1 tablespoon glucose syrup
2 tablespoons powdered gelatine
70 g (2½ oz/2 large) egg whites, at room temperature
2 tablespoons apple juice concentrate (see Notes)
½ teaspoon five-spice powder (see Notes)
Coloured sanding sugar to decorate (see Notes)

NOTES

Keep in an airtight container for 2–3 days.

If five-spice powder is not to your liking, substitute equal amounts of mixed (pumpkin pie) spice and cinnamon.

Apple juice concentrate is available in the health food aisle of supermarkets.

Sanding sugar is available from specialty cake decorating stores or online.

Japanese Green Tea Marshmallows with Black Sesame

MAKES ABOUT 34

515 g (1 lb 2½ oz/2¼ cups)
    caster (superfine) sugar
1 tablespoon glucose syrup
1½ tablespoons Japanese
    green tea powder
    (see Notes)
2 tablespoons powdered
    gelatine
70 g (2½ oz/2 large) egg
    whites, at room temperature
3 tablespoons black
    sesame seeds

COATING

2 tablespoons icing
    (confectioners') sugar
2 tablespoons cornflour
    (cornstarch)

NOTES

*Keep in an airtight container
for 2–3 days.*

*Green tea powder, also known
as 'matcha', is a fine powder
sold in pouches from Asian
grocery stores and specialty
tea shops.*

*Add a little green food
colouring if you would like to
intensify the 'green tea' colour.*

- Lightly spray a 20 x 30 cm (8 x 12 in) slice tin with oil, line the base and two long sides with non-stick baking paper and lightly spray the paper with oil.

- Combine 460 g (1 lb ¼ oz/2 cups) of the sugar, the glucose and 185 ml (6¼ fl oz/¾ cup) water in a small, deep heavy-based saucepan. Stir over low heat until the sugar dissolves. Bring to the boil and simmer, without stirring, until the syrup reaches 127°C (260°F) on a sugar thermometer (this is the upper end of the hard-ball stage). Watch it carefully, as the syrup has a tendency to bubble up.

- Meanwhile, combine the green tea powder with 1 tablespoon hot water in a microwave-safe bowl, then add enough cold water to make 185 ml (6¼ fl oz/¾ cup). Slowly sprinkle the gelatine over the tea and set aside for 5 minutes. Heat in the microwave for 30–45 seconds on High (100%), or until the gelatine has dissolved.

- When the sugar syrup reaches 115°C (239°F), whisk the egg whites in an electric mixer with a whisk attachment on medium speed. When frothy, increase the speed to medium–high and gradually add the remaining sugar, whisking until thick and glossy. Keep the mixer running on medium speed.

- When the sugar syrup reaches 127°C (260°F), turn off the heat. When the bubbles subside, carefully add the dissolved gelatine – take care, as the mixture may bubble up.

- Increase the mixer speed to medium–high and gradually pour the hot syrup mixture down the inside of the bowl in a thin, steady stream. Increase the speed to high and continue whisking until the mixture is very thick and holds its shape, about 10–12 minutes, depending on your mixer. The outside of the bowl should almost be at room temperature. Gently fold through 2 tablespoons of the sesame seeds, stirring and lifting the mixture only 2–3 times.

- Use a spatula to scrape the marshmallow mixture into the prepared tin and smooth the surface. Sprinkle with the remaining sesame seeds. Stand for 2–3 hours, until set.

- Meanwhile, to make the coating, sift the icing sugar and cornflour together.

- Turn the marshmallow out onto a clean surface. Dust the bottom with some of the coating. Use a large knife sprayed lightly with oil to cut the marshmallow into bite-sized pieces. Toss the marshmallow pieces in the remaining coating, dusting off the excess.

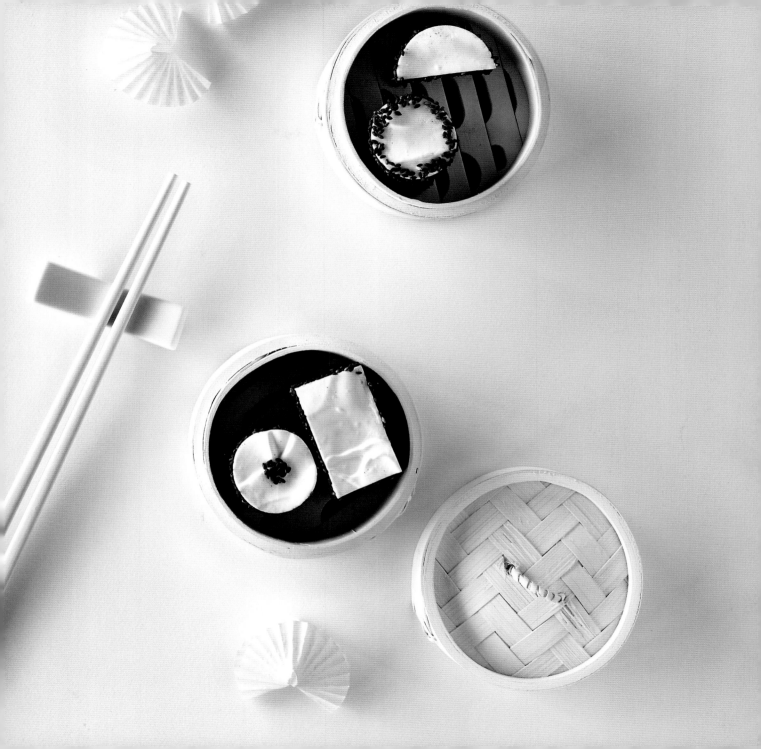

Sesame & Soy Marshmallows

MAKES ABOUT 35 MEDIUM OR 70 SMALL

- Lightly spray a 25 x 30 cm (10 x 12 in) baking tin with oil, line the base and two long sides with non-stick baking paper and lightly spray the paper with oil.

- Combine 460 g (1 lb ¼ oz/2 cups) of the sugar, the glucose and 185 ml (6¼ fl oz/¾ cup) water in a small, deep heavy-based saucepan. Stir over low heat until the sugar dissolves. Bring to the boil and simmer, without stirring, until the syrup reaches 127°C (260°F) on a sugar thermometer (this is the upper end of the hard-ball stage). Watch it carefully, as the syrup has a tendency to bubble up.

- Meanwhile, slowly sprinkle the gelatine over 185 ml (6¼ fl oz/¾ cup) cold water in a shallow microwave-safe bowl and set aside for 5 minutes. Heat in the microwave for 30–45 seconds on High (100%), or until the gelatine has dissolved and the liquid is clear.

- When the sugar syrup reaches 115°C (239°F), whisk the egg whites in an electric mixer with a whisk attachment on medium speed. When frothy, increase the speed to medium–high and gradually add the remaining sugar, whisking until thick and glossy. Keep the mixer running on medium speed.

- When the sugar syrup reaches 127°C (260°F), turn off the heat. When the bubbles subside, carefully add the dissolved gelatine – take care, as the mixture may bubble up.

- Increase the mixer speed to medium–high and gradually pour the hot syrup mixture down the inside of the bowl in a thin, steady stream. Increase the speed to high and continue whisking until the mixture is thick. Add the soy sauce and whisk until the mixture is very thick and holds its shape, about 10–12 minutes, depending on your mixer. The outside of the bowl should almost be at room temperature.

- Use a spatula to scrape the marshmallow mixture into the prepared tin and smooth the surface. Stand for 2–3 hours, until set.

- Meanwhile, to make the coating, sift the icing sugar and cornflour together. Combine the sesame seeds in a separate bowl.

- Dust the top of the marshmallow lightly with some of the coating and turn out onto a clean surface. Dust the bottom lightly with more coating. Use a large knife or small round cutter sprayed lightly with oil to cut the marshmallow into pieces. Roll the sticky sides of each marshmallow piece in the seeds.

515 g (1 lb 2½ oz/2¼ cups) caster (superfine) sugar

1 tablespoon glucose syrup

2 tablespoons powdered gelatine

70 g (2½ oz/2 large) egg whites, at room temperature

4–5 teaspoons good-quality soy sauce

SESAME COATING

2 tablespoons icing (confectioners') sugar

2 tablespoons cornflour (cornstarch)

40 g (1½ oz/¼ cup) white sesame seeds, toasted

40 g (1½ oz/¼ cup) black sesame seeds

NOTES

Keep in an airtight container for 2–3 days.

Soy sauce may seem an unusual choice for a marshmallow flavouring, but the sugar in the marshmallow mixture brings out its caramel tones. Give it a go, it's amazing!

Pomegranate Marshmallows with Pistachio Praline

MAKES ABOUT 20

515 g (1 lb 2½ oz/2¼ cups) caster (superfine) sugar

1 tablespoon glucose syrup

2 tablespoons powdered gelatine

70 g (2½ oz/2 large) egg whites, at room temperature

80 ml (2¾ fl oz/⅓ cup) pomegranate molasses (see Notes)

Pink food colouring, if desired

PISTACHIO PRALINE

110 g (3¾ oz/¾ cup) shelled pistachio nuts, lightly toasted

165 g (5¾ oz/¾ cup) sugar

COATING

2 tablespoons icing (confectioners') sugar

2 tablespoons cornflour (cornstarch)

NOTES

Keep in an airtight container for 2–3 days (roll in praline just before serving).

Pomegranate molasses is available from Middle Eastern and gourmet food stores.

• Lightly spray a 25 x 30 cm (10 x 12 in) baking tin with oil, line the base and two long sides with non-stick baking paper and lightly spray the paper with oil. Combine 460 g (1 lb ¼ oz/2 cups) of the sugar, the glucose and 185 ml (6¼ fl oz/¾ cup) water in a small, deep heavy-based saucepan. Stir over low heat until the sugar dissolves. Bring to the boil and simmer, without stirring, until the syrup reaches 127°C (260°F) on a sugar thermometer (this is the upper end of the hard-ball stage). Watch it carefully, as the syrup has a tendency to bubble up.

• Meanwhile, slowly sprinkle the gelatine over 185 ml (6¼ fl oz/¾ cup) cold water in a shallow microwave-safe bowl and set aside for 5 minutes. Heat in the microwave for 30–45 seconds on High (100%), or until the gelatine has dissolved.

• When the sugar syrup reaches 115°C (239°F), whisk the egg whites in an electric mixer with a whisk attachment on medium speed. When frothy, increase the speed to medium–high and gradually add the remaining sugar, whisking until thick and glossy. Keep the mixer running on medium speed. When the sugar syrup reaches 127°C (260°F), turn off the heat. When the bubbles subside, carefully add the dissolved gelatine – take care, as the mixture may bubble up.

• Increase the mixer speed to medium–high and gradually pour the hot syrup mixture down the inside of the bowl in a thin, steady stream. Increase the speed to high and continue whisking until the mixture is thick. Add the pomegranate molasses, a tablespoon at a time, and whisk until the mixture is very thick and holds its shape, about 10–12 minutes, depending on your mixer. The outside of the bowl should almost be at room temperature. Use a spatula to scrape the marshmallow mixture into the prepared tin and smooth the surface. Stand for 2–3 hours, until set.

• Meanwhile, to make the coating, sift the icing sugar and cornflour together. To make the pistachio praline, spread the pistachios over a tray lined with non-stick baking paper. Combine the sugar and 60 ml (2 fl oz/¼ cup) water in a saucepan. Stir over low heat until the sugar dissolves, brushing the sides of the pan with a clean pastry brush dipped in water to dissolve any crystals that may have formed. Bring to the boil and cook, without stirring, until the syrup is golden. Immediately pour over the pistachio nuts to cover. Allow to set, then finely chop the praline. Store in an airtight container.

• Dust the top and bottom of the marshmallow with some of the coating. Just before serving, use a flower-shaped cutter sprayed lightly with oil to cut the marshmallow into shapes. Roll the sticky sides of each marshmallow piece in the praline.

Rose Marshmallows

MAKES ABOUT 35 MEDIUM OR DOZENS OF SMALL

- Lightly spray a 25 x 30 cm (10 x 12 in) baking tin with oil, line the base and two long sides with non-stick baking paper and spray the paper with oil.

- Combine 460 g (1 lb ¼ oz/2 cups) of the sugar, the glucose and 185 ml (6¼ fl oz/¾ cup) water in a small, deep heavy-based saucepan. Stir over low heat until the sugar dissolves. Bring to the boil and simmer, without stirring, until the syrup reaches 127°C (260°F) on a sugar thermometer (this is the upper end of the hard-ball stage). Watch it carefully, as the syrup has a tendency to bubble up.

- Meanwhile, slowly sprinkle the gelatine over 185 ml (6¼ fl oz/¾ cup) cold water in a shallow microwave-safe bowl and set aside for 5 minutes. Heat in the microwave for 30–45 seconds on High (100%), or until the gelatine has dissolved and the liquid is clear.

- When the sugar syrup reaches 115°C (239°F), whisk the egg whites in an electric mixer with a whisk attachment on medium speed. When frothy, increase the speed to medium–high and gradually add the remaining sugar, whisking until thick and glossy. Keep the mixer running on medium speed.

- When the sugar syrup reaches 127°C (260°F), turn off the heat. When the bubbles subside, carefully add the dissolved gelatine – take care, as the mixture may bubble up.

- Increase the mixer speed to medium–high and gradually pour the hot syrup mixture down the inside of the bowl in a thin, steady stream. Increase the speed to high and continue whisking until the mixture is thick. Add the rosewater and a few drops of food colouring and whisk until the mixture is very thick and holds its shape, about 10–12 minutes, depending on your mixer. The outside of the bowl should almost be at room temperature.

- Use a spatula to scrape the marshmallow mixture into the prepared tin and smooth the surface. Stand for 2–3 hours until set.

- Meanwhile, to make the coating, sift the icing sugar and cornflour together.

- Turn the marshmallow out onto a clean surface. Use small round cutters or a large knife sprayed lightly with oil to cut the marshmallow into bite-sized pieces. Toss half of the marshmallows in the coating mixture, dusting off the excess. Toss the remaining marshmallows in the rose petals.

515 g (1 lb 2½ oz/2¼ cups) caster (superfine) sugar
1 tablespoon glucose syrup
2 tablespoons powdered gelatine
70 g (2½ oz/2 large) egg whites, at room temperature
¾ teaspoon rosewater, or to taste (see Notes)
Pink food colouring
Dried rose petals to decorate (see Notes)

COATING

2 tablespoons icing (confectioners') sugar
2 tablespoons cornflour (cornstarch)

NOTES

Keep in an airtight container for 2–3 days.

Rose petals and rosewater are available from Middle Eastern or gourmet grocery stores. Rosewater varies in strength, so be careful not to overdo it.

For a swirled pattern, add a few extra drops of food colouring to the marshmallow mixture and fold through a couple of times before pouring it into the tin.

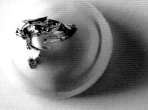

Saffron & Honey Marshmallows

MAKES ABOUT 50

2 good pinches saffron
  threads
400 g (14 oz/1¾ cups) caster
  (superfine) sugar
150 g (5½ oz) honey
2 tablespoons powdered
  gelatine
70 g (2½ oz/2 large) egg
  whites, at room temperature
Edible gold leaf to decorate

COATING
30 g (1 oz/¼ cup) icing
  (confectioners') sugar
30 g (1 oz/¼ cup) cornflour
  (cornstarch)

NOTE
*Keep in an airtight container
for 2–3 days.*

- Lightly spray 3 large trays with oil. Put the saffron in a shallow microwave-safe bowl and cover with 160 ml (5¼ fl oz/⅔ cup) warm water. Set aside to cool.

- Combine 345 g (12 oz/1½ cups) of the sugar, the honey and 125 ml (4 fl oz/½ cup) water in a medium, deep heavy-based saucepan. Stir over low heat until the sugar dissolves. Bring to the boil and simmer, without stirring, until the syrup reaches 127°C (260°F) on a sugar thermometer (this is the upper end of the hard-ball stage). Watch it carefully, as the syrup has a tendency to bubble up.

- Meanwhile, slowly sprinkle the gelatine over the saffron mixture and set aside for 5 minutes. Heat in the microwave for 30–45 seconds on High (100%), or until the gelatine has dissolved.

- When the sugar syrup reaches 115°C (239°F), whisk the egg whites in an electric mixer with a whisk attachment on medium speed. When frothy, increase the speed to medium–high and gradually add the remaining sugar, whisking until thick and glossy. Keep the mixer running on medium speed.

- When the sugar syrup reaches 127°C (260°F), turn off the heat and allow the bubbles to subside.

- Increase the mixer speed to medium–high and gradually pour the gelatine mixture down the inside of the bowl in a thin, steady stream. Add the hot sugar syrup in the same manner. Increase the speed to high and continue whisking until the mixture is very thick and holds its shape, about 12–14 minutes, depending on your mixer. The outside of the bowl should almost be at room temperature. Scrape the whisk attachment with a spatula to remove the saffron threads that have caught there, and fold them back into the mixture.

- Spoon dollops of the marshmallow mixture onto the oiled trays. Stand for 1–2 hours, until set.

- Meanwhile, to make the coating, sift the icing sugar and cornflour together. Dust the marshmallows very lightly with coating, dusting off the excess. Using a small dry brush, very carefully dab a little gold leaf onto each marshmallow.

CHAPTER 7

VARIETY

★ ★ ★

Choc Peanut Wagon Wheels

MAKES ABOUT 50

1 quantity Citrus marshmallow
    mixture (page 102)
1 teaspoon vanilla bean paste
80 g (2¾ oz/¼ cup)
    raspberry jam
200 g (7 oz) dark chocolate,
    melted
160 g (5½ oz/1 cup) roasted
    salted peanuts, chopped

CHOCOLATE
SHORTBREAD COOKIES

175 g (6 oz) unsalted butter,
    softened
80g (2¾ oz/⅓ cup, firmly
    packed) dark brown sugar
260 g (9¼ oz/1¾ cups)
    plain (all-purpose) flour
30 g (1 oz/¼ cup) Dutch
    (unsweetened) cocoa powder

- Lightly spray a 25 x 30 cm (10 x 12 in) baking tin with oil, line the base and two long sides with non-stick baking paper and lightly spray the paper with oil. Preheat the oven to 150°C (300°F). Line 2 large baking trays with non-stick baking paper.

- Prepare the marshmallow mixture as instructed, omitting the orange zest and replacing it with the vanilla bean paste. Use a spatula to scrape the mixture into the prepared tin and smooth the surface. Stand for about 1 hour, until set.

- Meanwhile, to make the cookies, use an electric mixer with a paddle attachment to beat the butter and sugar for 8 minutes, until creamy. Add the sifted flour and cocoa in 2 batches and beat until just combined. Knead lightly to bring the dough together. Divide in half and roll between sheets of non-stick baking paper until 4–5 mm (¼ in) thick. Cut into rounds using a 7 cm (2¾ in) cutter, re-rolling the dough as necessary to make 24 cookies. Place the cookies on the lined trays, 2 cm (¾ in) apart. Bake for 25–30 minutes, swapping the trays halfway through cooking, until cooked through. Remove from the oven and cool on the trays.

- Spread ½ teaspoon of the jam over each cooled cookie, leaving a 1 cm (½ in) border. Use a 7 cm (2¾ in) cutter sprayed lightly with oil to cut the marshmallow into 12 rounds. Place the rounds on 12 of the cookies, then top with the remaining cookies. Use the back of a small spoon to spread the melted chocolate around the edge of the wagon wheels. Roll in the chopped peanuts and place on a tray lined with non-stick baking paper to set.

NOTES

Keep in an airtight container for 2–3 days.

Try different flavours in your marshmallow, and roll the wagon wheels in different types of nuts. Mini wagon wheels would also be fun.

Citrus Marshmallow Roulade with Chocolate Ganache

SERVES 8–10

285 g (10 oz/1¼ cups)
caster (superfine) sugar
2 teaspoons glucose syrup
1 tablespoon powdered
gelatine
35 g (1¼ oz/1 large) egg
white, at room temperature
½ teaspoon finely grated
orange zest
Almond praline (page 52),
broken into shards

FILLING
125 ml (4 fl oz/½ cup)
thickened (whipping) cream
80 ml (2¾ fl oz/⅓ cup)
Easy lemon and lime curd
(page 37)

CHOCOLATE GANACHE
60 ml (2 fl oz/¼ cup)
thickened (whipping) cream
100 g (3½ oz) dark
chocolate, chopped

NOTES
*May be refrigerated, but is best
eaten on the day it is made.*

*You can use good-quality
ready-made lemon curd in this
recipe if you like.*

• Lightly spray a 25 x 30 cm (10 x 12 in) baking tin with oil, line the base and two long sides with non-stick baking paper and lightly spray the paper with oil. Set aside 2 tablespoons of the sugar. Combine the remaining sugar, the glucose and 80 ml (2¾ fl oz/⅓ cup) water in a small, deep heavy-based saucepan. Stir over low heat until the sugar dissolves. Bring to the boil and simmer, without stirring, until the syrup reaches 127°C (260°F) on a sugar thermometer (this is the upper end of the hard-ball stage). The amount of syrup is quite small, so ensure your thermometer is immersed in the syrup without touching the base of the pan.

• Meanwhile, slowly sprinkle the gelatine over 80 ml (2¾ fl oz/⅓ cup) cold water in a shallow microwave-safe bowl and set aside for 5 minutes. Heat in the microwave for 30–45 seconds on High (100%), or until the gelatine has dissolved.

• When the sugar syrup reaches 115°C (239°F), whisk the egg white in an electric mixer with a whisk attachment on medium speed. When frothy, increase the speed to medium–high and gradually add the reserved sugar, whisking until thick and glossy. Keep the mixer running on medium speed. When the sugar syrup reaches 127°C (260°F), turn off the heat. When the bubbles subside, carefully add the dissolved gelatine – take care, as the mixture may bubble up.

• Increase the mixer speed to medium–high and gradually pour the hot syrup mixture down the inside of the bowl in a thin, steady stream. Increase the speed to high and continue whisking until the mixture is thick. Add the orange zest and whisk until the mixture is very thick and holds its shape, about 8–10 minutes, depending on your mixer. The outside of the bowl should almost be at room temperature.

• Use a spatula to scrape the marshmallow mixture into the prepared tin and smooth the surface. Stand for 1–2 hours, until set.

• Meanwhile, to make the filling, whip the cream until firm peaks just form. Fold in the curd, then cover and refrigerate until required. To make the ganache, heat the cream in a small saucepan until it just comes to a simmer. Remove from the heat, add the chocolate and stir until smooth. Set aside at room temperature.

• Turn the marshmallow out onto a piece of non-stick baking paper lightly sprayed with oil, with a short side facing you. Spread the filling over the marshmallow, leaving a 5 cm (2 in) border on the short side furthest from you. Roll up the marshmallow, starting at the short side closest to you, to enclose the filling. Place on a serving plate, seam side down. Drizzle with the ganache and top with the praline shards.

Cosmopolitan Rocky Road

MAKES 20

1 quantity Cranberry
cosmopolitan marshmallow
(page 70, see Notes)
140 g (5 oz/1 cup) hazelnuts,
toasted and skinned
185 g (6½ oz/1¼ cups)
sweetened dried cranberries
500 g (1 lb 2 oz) great-
quality white chocolate
100 g (3½ oz) butter, chopped

- Lightly spray a 20 x 20 cm (8 x 8 in) cake tin with oil and line the base and two sides with non-stick baking paper.

- Prepare the marshmallow as instructed. Once set, turn out onto a clean surface and cut one-third of the slab into approximately 1 cm (½ in) pieces with a large knife sprayed lightly with oil. Keep the remaining marshmallow for another use. Gently toss the marshmallow, hazelnuts and 140 g (5 oz/1 cup) of the cranberries together in a large bowl.

- Break the chocolate into pieces and put in a microwave-safe bowl with the butter. Microwave, uncovered, on Medium (50%), stirring every minute, for 4–5 minutes or until melted and combined. Alternatively, melt in a heatproof bowl over a saucepan of simmering water. Do not let the chocolate get hot or it will melt the marshmallow.

- Use a spatula to scrape the chocolate mixture over the marshmallow mixture and mix gently until combined. Spoon into the prepared tin, sprinkle with the remaining cranberries and refrigerate for 2 hours, or until set. Remove from the tin and cut into squares.

NOTES

You need a third of a slab of Cranberry cosmopolitan marshmallow (page 70) for this recipe. Roll the remaining marshmallow in a coating of combined icing (confectioners') sugar and cornflour (cornstarch) and enjoy – it's delicious served simply, too.

May be stored, covered, in the refrigerator for up to a week.

Chocolate & Salted Caramel Fondue

SERVES 10–12

- Prepare the marshmallow as instructed, ensuring you allow plenty of time for it to set.

- To make the caramel, combine the sugar, glucose and 60 ml (2 fl oz/¼ cup) water in a medium saucepan over low heat. Cook, stirring, until the sugar dissolves, brushing the sides of the pan with a wet pastry brush to dissolve any crystals that may have formed. Increase the heat to high, bring to the boil and cook, without stirring, until the syrup is golden. Remove from the heat and carefully stir in the cream. Return to low heat and add the butter, 1 piece at a time, whisking until combined. Whisk in the salt. Pour into a small heatproof bowl and keep warm.

- To make the chocolate fondue, put the chocolate and cream in a small saucepan over low heat. Cook, stirring, for 4–5 minutes or until smooth. Remove from the heat and stir in the Cointreau, if using. Pour into a small bowl.

- Serve the salted caramel and fondue with marshmallows and fruit for dipping.

NOTES

Choose your favourite marshmallows to dunk in these indulgent sauces.

Try other fruit, such as pineapple, mandarin, banana or raspberries.

1 quantity Classic vanilla
  marshmallow mixture
  (page 8)
500 g (1 lb 2 oz) strawberries

SALTED CARAMEL
220 g (7¾ oz/1 cup) sugar
1 tablespoon glucose syrup
125 ml (4 fl oz/½ cup)
  thickened (whipping) cream
50 g (1¾ oz) butter, cubed
½ teaspoon fine sea salt flakes

CHOCOLATE FONDUE
200 g (7 oz) great-quality
  dark chocolate, chopped
125 ml (4 fl oz/½ cup)
  thickened (whipping) cream
1 tablespoon Cointreau
  liqueur (optional)

Deluxe Raspberry Rocky Road

MAKES 20

1 quantity Double raspberry marshmallow (page 22)
60 g (2¼ oz/1 cup) shredded coconut, toasted
160 g (5½ oz/1 cup) macadamia nuts, toasted
500 g (1 lb 2 oz) great-quality dark chocolate
100 g (3½ oz) butter, chopped

- Lightly spray a 20 x 20 cm (8 x 8 in) cake tin with oil and line the base and two sides with non-stick baking paper.

- Prepare the marshmallow as instructed. Once set, turn out onto a clean surface and cut one-third of the slab into approximately 1 cm (½ in) pieces with a large knife sprayed lightly with oil. Keep the remaining marshmallow for another use. Toss the marshmallow and coconut in a large bowl until the marshmallow is coated. Add the nuts.

Break the chocolate into pieces and put in a microwave-safe bowl with the butter. Microwave, uncovered, on Medium (50%), stirring every minute, for 4–5 minutes or until melted and combined. Alternatively, melt in a heatproof bowl over a saucepan of simmering water. Do not let the chocolate get hot or it will melt the marshmallow.

- Pour the chocolate mixture over the marshmallow mixture and mix gently until combined. Spoon into the prepared tin and refrigerate for 2 hours, or until set. Remove from the tin and cut into squares.

NOTES

You will need a third of a slab of Double raspberry marshmallow (page 22) for this recipe. You could serve the remaining marshmallow with Chocolate and salted caramel fondue (page 107) or simply coat with combined icing (confectioners') sugar and cornflour (cornstarch) and enjoy it as is.

May be stored, covered, in the refrigerator for up to a week.

Grasshopper Pie

300 ml (10 fl oz) thickened (whipping) cream, plus extra to serve (optional)

1 quantity Citrus marshmallow mixture (page 102)

80 ml (2¾ fl oz/⅓ cup) milk

1 tablespoon crème de menthe liqueur

1 tablespoon white crème de cacao liqueur

Green food colouring

Sugar bugs or chocolate curls to decorate (see Notes)

COOKIE BASE

250 g (8½ oz/2¼ cups) chocolate ripple cookies, processed to crumbs

125 g (4½ oz) butter, melted

- Spray a 26 cm (10½ in) fluted loose-based flan tin with oil.

- To make the base, combine the cookie crumbs and butter. Press into the base of the oiled tin, then refrigerate until firm. Whip the cream until firm peaks just form, then cover and refrigerate until required.

- Prepare the marshmallow mixture as instructed, dissolving the gelatine in the milk instead of water. Omit the orange zest and carefully fold in the liqueurs when the marshmallow is thick. Ensure you beat the marshmallow mixture until it has reached room temperature or you will melt the cream. Use a large spoon or spatula to gently fold the whipped cream and a few drops of food colouring into the marshmallow mixture.

- Remove the base from the fridge and carefully loosen it in the tin. Use a spatula to scrape the marshmallow mixture into the base and refrigerate for 1–2 hours, until set. Decorate with chocolate curls and serve with extra cream, if desired.

NOTES

Sugar bugs are available from specialty cake decorating stores or online.

Peanut Butter & Jelly Marshmallow Squares

MAKES 20

1 quantity Citrus marshmallow mixture (page 102)
90 g (3¼ oz/⅓ cup) crunchy peanut butter
40 g (1½ oz) natural raspberry flavour jelly

COOKIE BASE
125 g (4½ oz) milk coffee cookies, processed to crumbs
80 g (2¾ oz) butter, melted

- Lightly spray a 20 x 20 cm (8 x 8 in) cake tin with oil. Line the base with non-stick baking paper, extending the paper up and over two opposite sides. Spray the paper lightly with oil.

- To make the base, combine the cookie crumbs and butter. Press into the base of the prepared tin, then refrigerate until firm.

- Prepare the marshmallow mixture as instructed, omitting the orange zest. While the marshmallow is whipping, warm the peanut butter in a small microwave-safe bowl in the microwave on Medium (50%) in 15-second bursts until softened slightly, but not hot.

- When the marshmallow is ready, spoon about half into a separate bowl. Add the softened peanut butter and fold with a large spoon or spatula to gently combine. Return this mixture to the remaining marshmallow and fold through, stirring and lifting the mixture only 2–3 times. Spoon over the prepared base. The mixture will be slightly swirled. Stand for about 30 minutes.

- Meanwhile, prepare the jelly following the packet instructions. Cool slightly, then pour into a shallow dish and refrigerate until the jelly starts to thicken to a consistency similar to egg white. Pour over the marshmallow and refrigerate for 2–3 hours, until set. Remove from the tin and cut into squares.

NOTES

May be stored, covered, in the refrigerator for 3–4 days.

For a real American twist on this recipe, use grape-flavoured jelly.

Raspberry Marshmallow Mess

SERVES 6–8

- Prepare the marshmallow as instructed. Once set, turn out onto a clean surface and cut one-third of the slab into approximately 1 cm (½ in) pieces with a large knife sprayed lightly with oil. Keep the remaining marshmallow for another use.

- Place half the strawberries in a large bowl and roughly mash. Add the marshmallow, raspberries, sugar, brandy and remaining strawberries. Stir well and set aside to macerate.

- Beat the cream and yoghurt until firm peaks just form. Do not over-beat. Gently fold in two-thirds of the marshmallow mixture. Layer in individual serving glasses with pieces of meringue and the remaining marshmallow mixture. Serve immediately.

NOTES

You will need a third of a slab of Double raspberry marshmallow (page 22) for this recipe. You could serve the remaining marshmallow with Chocolate and salted caramel fondue (page 107) or simply coat with combined icing (confectioners') sugar and cornflour (cornstarch) and enjoy it as is.

1 quantity Double raspberry marshmallow (page 22, see notes)

500 g (1 lb 2 oz) strawberries, hulled and halved

125 g (4½ oz) fresh or frozen (thawed) raspberries

55 g (2 oz/¼ cup) caster (superfine) sugar

2–3 tablespoons brandy, to taste

300 ml (10 fl oz) thickened (whipping) cream

160 ml (5¼ fl oz/⅔ cup) thick Greek-style yoghurt

50 g (1¾ oz) meringues, roughly chopped

Raspberry Shortbread Kisses

MAKES ABOUT 50

- Preheat the oven to 170°C (340°F). Line 2 large baking trays with non-stick baking paper.

- To make the cookies, use an electric mixer to beat the butter, icing sugar and lemon zest until smooth. Add the sifted flours. Stir to combine, then knead lightly until smooth. Roll out the dough between sheets of non-stick baking paper until it is 5 mm (¼ in) thick. Cut into rounds using a 4 cm (1½ in) cutter, re-rolling the dough as necessary. Place the cookies on the lined trays, 2 cm (¾ in) apart. Bake for 15–20 minutes, until lightly golden. Remove from the oven and cool on the trays.

- Meanwhile, to make the coating, sift the icing sugar and cornflour together.

- Prepare the marshmallow mixture as instructed, omitting the orange zest and replacing it with the colouring and flavouring. Ensure the mixture is very thick.

- Transfer the marshmallow mixture to a large piping bag fitted with a plain 10 mm (½ in) nozzle. Pipe 'kisses' of marshmallow onto each cookie. Stand for 1–2 hours, until set. Dust very lightly with coating, if desired.

NOTES

Keep in an airtight container for 1–2 days.

Raspberry oil flavouring is available from specialty cake decorating stores or online.

Chocolate fans may like to spread each cookie with a little melted chocolate before piping the marshmallow kisses.

1 quantity Citrus marshmallow mixture (page 102)
A few drops of pink food colouring
A few drops of raspberry oil flavouring (see Notes)

SHORTBREAD COOKIES

125 g (4½ oz) butter, softened
85 g (3 oz/⅔ cup) icing (confectioners') sugar
1 teaspoon finely grated lemon zest
150 g (5½ oz/1 cup) plain (all-purpose) flour
30 g (1 oz/¼ cup) cornflour (cornstarch)

COATING (OPTIONAL)

1 tablespoon icing (confectioners') sugar
1 tablespoon cornflour (cornstarch)

Wicked Hot Chocolate with Churros-Style Marshmallows

SERVES 6

1 quantity Citrus marshmallow
  mixture (page 102)
600 ml (21 fl oz) milk
200 g (7 oz) dark chocolate,
  chopped
185 ml (6¼ fl oz/¾ cup) cream
1 vanilla bean, split lengthwise
  and seeds scraped
1 cinnamon stick
1–2 tablespoons caster
  (superfine) sugar, to taste
1 whole star anise

SPICE SUGAR
1 whole star anise
80 g (2¾ oz/⅓ cup) caster
  (superfine) sugar
½ teaspoon ground cinnamon

- Lightly spray 2 large trays with oil. Prepare the marshmallow mixture as instructed, ensuring it is very thick and holding its shape well. Immediately transfer to a large piping bag fitted with a large star nozzle. Pipe the marshmallow into lengths of about 12 cm (4½ in), continuing until all the mixture has been used. Stand for 1–2 hours, or until set.

- To make the spice sugar, use a mortar and pestle or spice grinder to grind the star anise to a powder. Combine, to taste, with the sugar and cinnamon. When the marshmallow lengths are set, toss in the spice sugar to coat.

- For the hot chocolate, combine the milk, chocolate, cream, vanilla bean and seeds, cinnamon, sugar and the whole star anise in a medium, heavy-based saucepan over low heat. Warm the mixture, stirring continuously, until the chocolate has melted and the mixture is smooth. Remove the spices, pour into mugs and serve with the marshmallows for dipping.

Published in 2012 by Hardie Grant Books

Hardie Grant Books (Australia)
Ground Floor, Building 1
658 Church Street
Richmond, Victoria 3121
www.hardiegrant.com.au

Hardie Grant Books (UK)
Dudley House, North Suite
34–35 Southampton Street
London WC2E 7HF
www.hardiegrant.co.uk

A Cataloguing-in-Publication entry is available from the catalogue
of the National Library of Australia at www.nla.gov.au
The Artisan Marshmallow
ISBN 9781742704524

Publishing Director: Paul McNally
Design Manager: Heather Menzies
Designer: Allison Colpoys
Recipe text: Caroline Jones
Editor: Anna Goode
Photographer: Alicia Taylor
Stylist: Vicki Valsamis

The publisher would like to thank Specklefarm
(www.specklefarm.com.au) and Paper Eskimo
(www.papereskimo.com.au) for their assistance
in the photography of this book.

Colour reproduction by Splitting Image Colour Studio
Printed and bound in China by 1010 Printing International Limited